WHY JESUS

A 50-Day HOLY SPIRIT Experience

Alisa Hope Wagner

WHY JESUS

A 50-Day HOLY SPIRIT Experience

Why Jesus: A 50-Day Holy Spirit Experience
Copyright @ 2019 by Alisa Hope Wagner
All rights reserved
Marked Writers Publishing
www.alisahopewagner.com

Scriptures taken from various translations of the Bible found at www.biblegateway.com

---

Cover design by Alisa Hope Wagner
Author photo by Lori Stead of www.wetsilver.com

ISBN-13: 978-1-7334333-1-0
ISBN-10: 1-7334333-1-7

Dedication

Daniel – the man of my dreams

Isaac Jeremiah – my prophet

Levi Daniel – my shepherd

Karis Ruth – my graceful companion

Editing Team – Dave Cotham, Patricia Coughlin, Sam Faulkner, Faith Newton, Holly Smith, Daniel Wagner and Bernadine Zimmerman

Holy Spirit – my writing partner

"Then John testified, 'I saw the Holy Spirit descending like a dove from heaven and resting upon Him'" (John 1.32 NLT).

FOREWORD

I've had the honor and privilege to be able to watch Alisa Hope Wagner continue to grow in her walk with Christ, and as an author over the past decade or so. I distinctly remember a dinner with my wife and I, Alisa and her amazing husband Daniel, as we talked and prayed over her burning desire to publish her first book. Alisa knew deep in her spirit that God had a plan for her life and that He had gifted her, (and burdened her) with the skills and talents of an author. But we all recognized that it would be in God's timing, and in the interim all Alisa could do would be to wait, stay faithful and obedient, and continue doing what she loved, write!

It's so amazing to now see the fruits of Alisa's labors being poured out so fluently as she authors and publishes books on a regular basis. Her fictional works reflect her adventurous spirit as they engage readers, propelling them into the world of her characters, where life lessons are learned by the characters, and by the readers. Alisa's works that delve into the Christian faith are all enlightening and inspiring.

Why Jesus takes Alisa's passion for Christ and the indwelling of the Holy Spirit into a realm that will encourage and empower readers. You can feel the Spirit's leading in her words as Alisa walks us through a 50-day journey, reminding us of the sweet truths of the Gospel, the sanctification of our souls, and the manifestation of the Holy Spirit in our lives. Written in a Bible study format, *Why Jesus* will prove to be excellent for individual or group study. It will not only lift readers to a new spiritual level, it will leave them thirsting, for more of the Spirit, and for more of Alisa's writings.

I can't wait for you to be inspired as you take in *Why Jesus*, and I can't wait to see how God continues to use Alisa Hope Wagner as one of His instruments of faith.

Pastor Dave Cotham

Dave Cotham is the Executive Director for Majesty Outdoors. Majesty Outdoors is a non-profit organization fully committed to raising awareness to the fatherless epidemic facing our country and offering a solution through their TideChangers Mentorship program.

Dave served on the pastoral team at Church Unlimited, formerly Bay Area Fellowship, for 10 years. His role as Executive Pastor of Spiritual Development included leading the Life Groups ministry, God Behind Bars prison ministry, Celebrate Recovery, and developing curriculum for Bible studies and discipleship classes. Dave also helped launch and then pastor the Padre Island campus for Church Unlimited for 8 years.

Introduction

Jesus was crucified on Passover, but the Holy Spirit did not reveal Himself until Pentecost. There are 50 days between Passover (Jesus' death) to Pentecost (the Holy Spirit's entrance). During that time, the entire world had to wait for the Holy Spirit to finally dwell among and within us.

"But the Advocate, the Holy Spirit, whom the Father will send in my name, will teach you all things and will remind you of everything I have said to you" (John 14.26 NIV).

Jesus became the Passover Lamb, covering all God's children with His blood, saving us from eternal death—eternal separation from God. Just like the first Passover when the Israelites were enslaved in Egypt, God painted each of us with the blood of His Son, so His Spirit of Judgment would pass over our sin, allowing us to have a relationship with Him.

"On that same night I will pass through Egypt and strike down every firstborn of both people and animals, and I will bring judgment on all the gods of Egypt. I am the LORD. The blood will be your sign on the houses where you live. Whenever I see the blood, I'll pass over you. No

plague will destroy you when I strike the land of Egypt" (Exodus 12.12-13 NIV).

Pentecost is a Greek word that means "the Fiftieth Day." This was a holiday, called Feast of Weeks or *Shavuot* in Hebrew, celebrating God's provision in the harvest. After Jesus' death, resurrection and ascension back to the right hand of God, the disciples gathered in a house praying and waiting. Finally, the promised Holy Spirit came down like wind and fire, bringing God's power into the lives of people covered by the Lamb's blood.

"When the day of Pentecost came, they were all together in one place. Suddenly a sound like the blowing of a violent wind came from heaven and filled the whole house where they were sitting. They saw what seemed to be tongues of fire that separated and came to rest on each of them. All of them were filled with the Holy Spirit and began to speak in other tongues as the Spirit enabled them" (Acts 2.1-4 NIV).

The Holy Spirit flooded the disciples, and they spilled onto the streets with the Good News of Salvation through Jesus Christ. Three thousand people were saved that day. History from that moment would be forever changed. Grace completed the Law, and Jesus unleashed forgiveness and reconciliation onto the world. The Holy Spirit could now dwell among us. We were no longer separated from God because of the finished work of Jesus Christ!

Now a precedent of completed time has been made. First, Jesus is discovered. Second, our faith is recovered. Third, the Holy Spirit is uncovered.

How is Jesus discovered? By a Father who has sent Him and by a people who seek Him.

How is our faith recovered? We first believe in Jesus by faith, but during a time of waiting, we recover faith on a deeper level.

How is the Holy Spirit uncovered? Our disbelief is like a lid on the Holy Spirit, but when disbelief is usurped by faith, the Holy Spirit's power is released.

The number 50 represents the fullness of the time from when Jesus is discovered until our faith is recovered. It is different for each of us and every situation. But this book is designed for a threefold purpose: 1) to reveal Jesus, so He can be **discovered**. 2) to encourage faith, so it can be **recovered**. 3) to release the Holy Spirit, so God's power can be **uncovered**.

Let's do it together. The Holy Spirit is just waiting to be uncovered in our lives, our situations, our health, our relationships, our finances, our struggles.... Let us lean into Jesus every day, allowing His face to come into direct contact with our own. Let us recover and build our sustaining faith, so the Holy Spirit can reveal His power and authority in our lives.

This Bible study can be completed over 50 days. Each day will include three sections: **First**, each day will have a devotional discovering Jesus along with three contemplative questions. **Second**, each day will have a section on recovering faith along with a meditation moment. **Third**, each day will have a section on uncovering the Holy Spirit along with a professing prayer. Finally, each day comes with a short video from Alisa Hope Wagner where she can chat with you face-to-face about each topic. Check out her Youtube channel under her handle, Alisa Hope Wagner, and find her Why Jesus: A 50 Day Holy Spirit Experience Playlist.

The goal of this Bible study is not to simply be a tool for encouragement. It's a tool for transformation. The process of reading, answering, meditating and praying each day will bring the insight from the mind and plant it deep within the heart, so that our beliefs, thoughts, words and actions will align themselves with God and His kingdom. Change does not happen overnight. It occurs little by little and day by day as we press into the glorious image of Jesus. Give God 50 days, and watch Him explode His presence into your life!

"And we all, who with unveiled faces contemplate the Lord's glory, are being transformed into His image with ever-increasing glory, which comes from the Lord, who is the Spirit" (2 Corinthians 3.18 NIV).

Why Jesus Videos

You can find Alisa's videos that complement the 50-day devotional Holy Spirit experience. The QR Code to the Why Jesus playlist is below.

Table of Contents

Why Jesus: Day 1 1
Why Jesus: Day 2 6
Why Jesus: Day 3 10
Why Jesus: Day 4 16
Why Jesus: Day 5 21
Why Jesus: Day 6 26
Why Jesus: Day 7 32
Why Jesus: Day 8 37
Why Jesus: Day 9 43
Why Jesus: Day 10 48
Why Jesus: Day 11 54
Why Jesus: Day 12 60
Why Jesus: Day 13 66
Why Jesus: Day 14 72
Why Jesus: Day 15 78
Why Jesus: Day 16 83
Why Jesus: Day 17 89

Why Jesus: Day 18 95
Why Jesus: Day 19 101
Why Jesus: Day 20 107
Why Jesus: Day 21 113
Why Jesus: Day 22 119
Why Jesus: Day 23 125
Why Jesus: Day 24 131
Why Jesus: Day 25 137
Why Jesus: Day 26 143
Why Jesus: Day 27 149
Why Jesus: Day 28 156
Why Jesus: Day 29 162
Why Jesus: Day 30 167
Why Jesus: Day 31 173
Why Jesus: Day 32 178
Why Jesus: Day 33 183
Why Jesus: Day 34 189
Why Jesus: Day 35 195
Why Jesus: Day 36 200
Why Jesus: Day 37 206
Why Jesus: Day 38 211
Why Jesus: Day 39 216

Why Jesus: Day 40 .... *220*
Why Jesus: Day 41 .... *224*
Why Jesus: Day 42 .... *229*
Why Jesus: Day 43 .... *234*
Why Jesus: Day 44 .... *240*
Why Jesus: Day 45 .... *244*
Why Jesus: Day 46 .... *250*
Why Jesus: Day 47 .... *256*
Why Jesus: Day 48 .... *262*
Why Jesus: Day 49 .... *268*
Why Jesus: Day 50 .... *274*

WHY JESUS: DAY 1

Jesus Discovered

"If only there were a mediator between us, someone who could bring us together" (Job 9.33 NLT).

People throughout time have always tried to be good enough in order to reach some kind of perfect state, so they could achieve oneness with God. Human religions offer us suggestions on how we might live and what we might do to achieve a higher spiritual stature. But a barrier, our flesh and the sin that dwells therein, prevents us from achieving this perfect state, and humans have written books, created movies and analyzed how men and women, in their own strength, can break down the wall that divides our body and spirit, our torment and peace. But no matter what we do or how we think and feel, we cannot in and of ourselves reach this higher place. Jumping from one dimension to another is impossible without a portal. Even when our bodies die, our sin separates us from a holy God. We cannot bridge the gap on our own. Jesus Christ is the only portal to God the Father. He is our ticket, our gift from God, so we can have access to Him. Once we are found in Christ, He can now break the barrier from the natural to the supernatural. We can now reach that higher state of perfection because Jesus is our mediator, uniting us back to God.

"Jesus answered, 'I am the way and the truth and the life. No one comes to the Father except through Me'" (John 14.6 NIV).

Contemplative Questions

1. Do you try in your own strength to be good enough for God? What are some ways you try?

2. Jesus is our only portal to God. Do you find this freeing or restricting? Why?

3. Grace means accepting something you didn't earn. Can you accept grace for the salvation you have been given as a free gift?

Faith Recovered

"The Lord blessed the latter part of Job's life more than the former part...." (Job 42.12a NIV).

The Book of Job in the Bible records the story of a man who had to recover his faith. When the story opens, God declares to Satan that Job is the most righteous man on earth. Satan scoffs, suggesting that Job is only blameless because he has everything he wants—riches, family and comforts. There is no struggle or need in Job's life. Therefore, God allows Satan to put Job through a season of testing to see whether Job's faith will rise to the occasion or if his faith dwindles and dies. Job struggles to understand why bad things happen to good people, but he finally comes to the conclusion that God is all good, despite his circumstances, and he cannot presume to understand God's ways. Job recovers His faith and receives a deeper revelation of God, and God intervenes with power, celebration and reward—blessing Job's life even more than before.

Meditation Moment

Imagine God in the Flesh, Jesus, in His glory, sitting at the right-hand side of God in His throne. Now envision a

Alisa Hope Wagner
WHY JESUS

beautiful spiritual umbilical cord, connecting you to Him. You are receiving all of His goodness and favor.

Holy Spirit Uncovered

"I believe that if I should preach to you the atonement of our Lord Jesus, and nothing else, twice every Sabbath day, my ministry would not be unprofitable. Perhaps it might be more profitable than it is." – Charles Spurgeon

The Holy Spirit is literally God's Spirit residing in the world. Normally, God's Spirit cannot dwell in anything imperfect or corrupt because God Himself is perfect and Holy. However, because of the finished work of Jesus Christ, all of earth and humanity are now seen as perfect and holy in God's eyes through the lens of Jesus' blood. The Bible says all of our good works are considered dirty rags compared to the awesome holiness of God (Isaiah 64.6). Does that mean we don't even try? No, because we know that Jesus Christ will redeem all of our work done in obedience to God. Jesus has made our filthy rags beautiful and pleasing to God.

Professing Prayer

"Father God, I know my works for You will never be good enough, but I also believe that Jesus is the perfecter of my life and work. I trust that all my obedience done in response to Your word has meaning and purpose and will be rewarded."

WHY JESUS: DAY 2

Jesus Discovered

"Look! The virgin will conceive a child! She will give birth to a Son, and they will call Him Immanuel, which means 'God is with us'" (Matthew 1.23 NLT).

The blood of Jesus Christ is the most important, yet the most perplexing truth of Jesus. Why blood? Why does such a seemingly gruesome thing play such a monumental role in our faith? The main lie to dispel is that blood is gruesome. Yes, the enemy would like to create counterfeits of the blood in movies, video games and other forms of entertainment. But blood is the life source of a living thing. For Jesus to give His life source in order to redeem the world is not gruesome—it is beautiful. The Blood of Jesus Christ is God in the flesh. It is Eternal Water rained down on the earth, merged into temporal existence and squeezed out onto the New Testament time that we live in, a time that prophets of old could only dream about. We have Emmanuel, God with us, because God poured out His Supernatural Spirit into a natural world. The blood passes through the umbilical cord of Christ, connecting God to His children who are still maturing in the womb of this earth. We feed from the life source of Jesus, filling our souls, minds, bodies and spirits with the very essence of our Creator God.

"This is the one who came by water and blood—Jesus Christ. He did not come by water only, but by water and blood. And it is the Spirit who testifies, because the Spirit is the truth" (1 John 5.6 NIV).

Contemplative Questions

1. God is with us. How does knowing that we have a Creator who walked this earth make Him feel closer and more accessible?

2. Does the blood of Jesus Christ sound gruesome or beautiful to you? Explain.

3. Jesus loves you so much that He died, spilling His blood, so He could have a relationship with you. How does knowing you are loved by God change your perception of your life?

Faith Recovered

"Christ is so in love with holiness, that at the price of His blood He will buy it for us." – John Flavel

Moses and the priests were called to sprinkle the people with the blood of the sacrifice (Exodus 24.8). In fact, the priests sprinkled the altar, tabernacle, ministry vessels, mercy seat, doorposts and more with blood. This image can seem gross and messy at first, but when we realize that the blood of Jesus is redemptive and restorative, the blood becomes a miraculous phenomenon that we want on everyone and everything. Everything in our life – family, marriage, friendships, work, leisure, study, etc.— can be offered to God. God loves us and He wants to be a part of every single aspect of our daily life. We can imagine Jesus' blood being sprinkled on each detail from the epic to the mundane.

Meditation Moment

Can you replace the Hollywood image of blood with the image that God designed? Take a moment to imagine the purifying blood of Jesus washing over every wound, sin and pain in your life. See the blood as the beautiful life source of God, restoring every aspect of your mind, body and soul.

Holy Spirit Uncovered

"Instead, one of the soldiers pierced Jesus' side with a spear, bringing a sudden flow of blood and water" (John 19.34 NIV).

Jesus' side was pierced after He died on the cross. Guess what came out? Blood and water. The water represents God's Spirit poured out onto the world. The blood represents God in the Flesh, or Immanuel, God with us. They are symbolically both poured out onto the world through the death of Jesus Christ. This is important because the Holy Spirit brings the very nature of God into our lives. We have God's goodness, provision and abundance through Jesus Christ once we receive Him into our hearts as our Lord and Savior. God will not force the Holy Spirit into our life, we must invite Him into every facet of who we are and what we do.

Professing Prayer

"Holy Spirit, I am aware of Your presence inside of my heart, soul, mind and body. Engulf me with Your warmth, favor and goodness. I give You all of my fears, worries and anxieties, and I choose to rest in Your goodness."

WHY JESUS: DAY 3

Jesus Discovered

"In Him we have redemption through His blood, the forgiveness of sins, in accordance with the riches of God's grace" (Ephesians 1.7 NIV).

The forgiveness of Jesus creates awe in us when we fully realize how powerful and all-encompassing this gift is. We have been forgiven completely and irrevocably. No matter our tattered souls and bodies. No matter our corrupted minds and thoughts. We can set the past on the cross and embrace fully the righteousness of Christ. We are righteous. We are holy. We are pure. We are whole. We are perfected in Christ. If we could only focus on that truth and allow the work of the Holy Spirit to deal with the rest, what peace and joy and contentment we could claim every single moment of our lives. His forgiveness is continuous, like a spring of healing water continuously lapping over our wounded soul. The proof of Jesus' forgiveness in our lives is the indwelling of the Holy Spirit (God's Spirit) in us. This intimacy would be impossible if sin separated us from God. The righteousness is there in the supernatural, so now it is time to work that righteousness into every area of our natural lives. Our soul is getting restored. Our mind is getting renewed. Our strength is getting refreshed. And our body is getting healed. All this healing is a response to the forgiveness of sin and the righteousness we now own through Jesus Christ.

"God has united you with Christ Jesus. For our benefit God made him to be wisdom itself. Christ made us right with God; He made us pure and holy, and He freed us from sin" (1 Corinthians 1.30 NLT).

Contemplative Questions

1. What areas in your life need healing? What is the first step the Holy Spirit has been prompting you to take toward restoration in one area?

2. Is there someone you need to forgive or ask forgiveness from? Will you contact that person today?

3. If the person you need to forgive is not available to you, imagine that person in front of you. Now envision the power of forgiveness filling you and reaching out to that person.

Faith Recovered

"Let us acknowledge the LORD; let us press on to acknowledge Him. As surely as the sun rises, He will appear; He will come to us like the winter rains, like the spring rains that water the earth" (Hosea 6.3 NIV).

There are two rains: the spring rains and the winter rains that fall on our God-given promises. The spring rain is when we receive God's promises. We are excited and the word is fresh, but we are ignorant to how truly impossible this promise is to achieve. After we have been given the initial promise, we go through a long season of obedience and waiting. We obediently work towards those promises and wait on the Lord, yet the promises seem to slowly die in the natural. It is at the moment of death that we have to reestablish our faith –not in blissful ignorance, but in the reality of impossibility. If we can cling to faith based on God's word alone no matter our situation, that is when our faith is recovered on a much deeper level.

Meditation Moment

Imagine your promises as a dry desert. You've been digging a deep hole searching for water. You want to give up, but you continued to dig. Finally, like rains bursting forth, you reach the water deep within the ground. Your promises receive the winter rain.

Holy Spirit Uncovered

"Just as water seeks to fill the lowest places, so God fills you with His glory and power when He finds you empty and abased." – Andrew Murray

The Holy Spirit is compared to living water (John 7.38). Jesus promises us that if we come to Him, He will give us "rivers of living water," flowing from our lives. The enemy of our hearts and life circumstances will do everything to make us focus on the dry desert surrounding us. We might be tempted to leave where God has called us to stay. The "hole" we've been digging in obedience seems to only get bigger, and the water will not spring forth. But don't give up. If God has already given us the spring rain of our promises, He will give us the winter rain—we just have to wait on His timing. Waiting can be distressing if we mistrust God. Or it can be peaceful if we trust God. We can choose to believe God at His word and endure the process with thanksgiving and praise.

Professing Prayer

"Holy Spirit, I am so tired. I've worked for so long obeying and waiting on You. But I know that You will come through. I know that You will let loose the winter rains on my promises. I will renew my faith in Your word. I believe

You no matter how dry and dead my circumstances seem."

WHY JESUS: DAY 4

Jesus Discovered

"Neither shall they say, Lo here! or, lo there! for, behold, the kingdom of God is within you" (Luke 17.21 KJV).

The struggle on this earth causes us to reach out to the supernatural, beyond the natural world, in search for God. Without God, there is no good, no perfection, no love, no peace and no joy. Since all of us have sinned, we are separated from God because He is perfectly holy. We live in an imperfect world filled with heartache, pain and sorrow. But it is our struggle that ignites our need for a savior. It is the imperfect womb of earth that gives us eternal eyes for heaven. Every heartache creates in us a desire for God's healing. Every pain creates in us a need for God's peace. Every sorrow creates in us a yearning for God's joy. Without these struggles, we would not cling onto Jesus. We grasp the cross, knowing that only through it can we attain God's goodness on earth. The Holy Spirit dwells in each person who has been saved by grace through the finished work of Jesus on the cross. We have heaven on earth because God's kingdom is in each of us.

"Not only that, but we rejoice in our sufferings, knowing that suffering produces endurance, and endurance produces character, and character produces hope, and hope does not put us to shame, because God's love has been poured into our hearts through the Holy Spirit who has been given to us" (Romans 5.3-5 ESV).

Contemplative Questions

1. What heartaches have caused you to cling onto the cross of Jesus?

2. Have there been times of plenty and comfort that lured you away from God?

3. Has God changed or strengthened you through struggle and/or adversity?

Faith Recovered

"He will wipe every tear from their eyes. There will be no more death or mourning or crying or pain, for the old order of things has passed away" (Revelation 21.4 NIV).

Life isn't fair and all people suffer. This is one of the hardest truths that we struggle with from a young age. We wonder why God would allow heartache and pain on this earth. As parents, our children will make decisions that hurt themselves and others, but does this knowledge prevent us from having children? Do we skip being mothers, fathers and mentors because we know that the ones we care for will make mistakes that hurt and cause pain? God knew we would corrupt His perfect creation by our sin, but He already had His redemptive plan in place—Jesus Christ. We can get through the troubles of today, knowing that they are only temporary.

Meditation Moment

Imagine being surrounded by a supernatural covering of heaven. The Holy Spirit within you is enveloping you in this covering. Whenever you feel stressed or the pains and troubles of this life press down on you, go into the covering of God and find a place of peace and joy with Him.

Holy Spirit Uncovered

"God dwells in His creation and is everywhere indivisibly present in all His works. He is transcendent above all his words even while He is immanent within them." – A. W. Tozer

Through Jesus Christ, the Holy Spirit is now in us. Unlike parents, siblings, friends, doctors and pastors, God never sleeps (Psalm 121.4). He is always available to us every moment of every day. And unlike people, God is always in the mood to chat with us about life, our feelings, our relationships, our struggles, etc. God sent His Son to die for us, so He can have this communication with us! Our ability to chat with God came at a high price, so we want to joyfully access it morning, noon and night! And we don't have to simply go to God for the big stuff we are dealing with, He wants to be involved in the small stuff, as well. God is in love with all of us, and He desires to be a part of every aspect of our daily life. He's just waiting for us to acknowledge Him and invite Him into our day.

Professing Prayer

"Holy Spirit, I know You are inside of me and all around me. Let me learn to turn towards You when I'm contemplating little and big problems. I want You to be an active member of my day."

WHY JESUS: DAY 5

Jesus Discovered

"For God, who said, 'Let there be light in the darkness,' has made this light shine in our hearts so we could know the glory of God that is seen in the face of Jesus Christ" (2 Corinthians 4.6 NLT).

When we become Christians, we are washed in the blood of Jesus, meaning our sins are cleansed by the redeeming essence of our God who became flesh in order to save and reconcile us back to Him. Every part of us is supernaturally clean, and the Holy Spirit is working that truth into every natural nook and cranny of our lives. However, as we follow the leading of the Holy Spirit, we will encounter the heartache of this world. We are the hands and feet of Jesus, and in us, He wants to reach the hurt and the broken. We will see and experience darkness, bringing light to those who are lost. Just like the disciples, our feet will become dirty from following Jesus down paths to the needy, and only He can refresh us and purify our hearts, minds and souls. That is why we must go to Him. He gives us the grace to see, hear and experience difficult things, but He is always there wiping away the grime and debris from our life of obedience to Him.

"Jesus answered, 'Those who have had a bath need only to wash their feet; their whole body is clean…'" (John 13.10 NIV).

Contemplative Questions

1. What part of your life tends to get grimy working with imperfect, wounded people?

2. Are you able to go to Jesus when you feel the dirt of service building up, as you faithfully obey Him?

3. When is the last time you rested in Jesus, allowing Him to refresh and restore you?

Faith Recovered

"Beware in your prayer, above everything, of limiting God, not only by unbelief, but by fancying that you know what he can do." – Andrew Murray

Jesus' disciples saw a lot of pain, sickness and heartache as they journeyed with Jesus. But during this time of ministry, they learned that there was great power in the very name of Jesus. The name of Jesus could heal the sick, cast away demonic forces and even raise the dead. However, the name couldn't just be used without belief. Jesus said that whoever uses His name would never be able to say anything bad about Him, which indicates a great love and respect (Mark 9.39). Only a heart truly in love and devoted to Jesus could fully experience the power of His name. The power of belief allows God to do more than we could ever think or imagine (Ephesians 3.20).

Meditation Moment

We learn about Jesus when we read the Bible. Try to envision everything you have learned about Jesus and apply it to His name. Jesus embodies love, mercy, forgiveness, power, authority, strength, goodness, wholeness, healing, etc. Speak the name Jesus over and

over again, attributing all of these powerful descriptions to His amazing name.

Holy Spirit Uncovered

"He could not do any miracles there, except lay His hands on a few sick people and heal them. He was amazed at their lack of faith" (Mark 6.5-6 NIV).

God's Spirit only flows out after Jesus' blood has made a way. If there is a breakthrough we are needing, and we want God to pour into a certain area, Jesus and His name are the catalyst. Have faith in the name of Jesus today. Don't be like Jesus' hometown who prevented the miracles because they lacked faith and took the name of Jesus for granted. See the power of His mighty blood paving a way for the Holy Spirit to enter our situation. God will make a way where this is no way. The Holy Spirit has the power to heal, restore, provide and overflow all of God's goodness and favor and grace into our lives. Jesus is the key to unlock the power of God's Spirit. Instead of constantly trying and trying in our own efforts, take a moment to simply pray, ask and believe.

Professing Prayer

"Holy Spirit, I believe in the name of Jesus. I believe that His blood makes a way for You to act powerfully in my life. I'm banking all of my faith on Jesus and not the works of my flesh. Help me to stop trying and start trusting."

WHY JESUS: DAY 6

Jesus Discovered

"And this gospel of the kingdom will be preached in all the world as a witness to all the nations, and then the end will come" (Matthew 24.14 NKJV).

Many times we think of an apostle as the twelve who followed Jesus, including the Apostle Paul who met Jesus after His ascension. We are afraid to give the name apostle to anyone, thinking it can only be designated to someone perfect, holy and sanctified. However, what we forget is that each of God's children, who have been saved by the work of Jesus Christ on the cross, has been made perfect, holy and sanctified. We too have the Holy Spirit within us Who yearns to reach a lost world. The Greek word, *Apostle,* was used in the Roman empire to signify an ambassador. It was designated to any Roman leader appointed to take new territory for the kingdom. This person would find foreign land and bring the culture, values and ideas of Rome to the people, adopting them and their land into the empire. We are all a part of the body of Christ, and God will call each of us to be an ambassador to a foreign land, bringing light into the dark places. We may not have the Office of Apostle, but we can definitely move in the gifting of apostleship. In our unique way, we can establish God's kingdom—whether with a new business, family, book, evangelical movement, etc.—bringing God's culture, values and ideas into all the far reaches of the earth.

"In the same way, let your light shine before others, that they may see your good deeds and glorify your Father in heaven" (Matthew 5.16 NIV).

Contemplative Questions

1. Do you feel like God is calling you into new territory?

2. How has God qualified you to take His presence into places that may seem difficult for others to reach?

3. Forging paths into unknown lands can be scary. Will you trust God with your steps even if the way isn't totally clear?

Faith Recovered

"The Christian experience, from start to finish, is a journey of faith." – Watchman Nee

Going into unknown territory is one of the scariest but most rewarding steps of faith a person can take. Just like the explorers of old, we each face the choice to stay in our comfortable circumstances or venture out into desolate lands and establish something new. *The first person through the wall gets the bloodiest* is a paraphrase of a famous quote, which means that when we become ambassadors for Jesus, we will be heavily attacked by Satan and anyone under his control. Satan does not want God's agenda to take ground, so he will pull out all the stops to prevent us from obeying God's command to explore with God. However, if God is calling us, He will equip us and prepare us for the journey. And when we think the enemy has beaten us, God will give us His strength, power and resources to continue walking faithfully with Him (1 Corinthians 10.13).

Meditation Moment

Can you imagine the territory God is calling you to explore with Him? There may be weeds of distractions, allowing the enemy to slither and hide in the shadows. But you

don't have to fear. Envision God clearing the path step by step with His mighty arm of strength.

Holy Spirit Uncovered

"The LORD himself goes before you and will be with you; He will never leave you nor forsake you. Do not be afraid; do not be discouraged" (Deuteronomy 31.8 NIV).

God is everywhere and has seen history from start to finish. He exists outside of time, so the fruition of His kingdom plan is stretched out before His all-knowing eyes. We live within the limits of time, so we can only see what is in front of us. Therefore, we can't allow our own point-of-view to guide us or else our lives will be severely limited. We must trust that although the territory seems new and scary, nothing surprises God. He knows exactly what lies ahead, and He sent us His Spirit to guide us. We can obey His call to be an ambassador for Him, and follow His lead one step at a time. Instead of fretting about what we don't see, we can be excited over all the possibilities that lie before us.

Professing Prayer

"Holy Spirit, I trust that You see the beginning to the end. I feel You sending me outside of my comfort zone. I know that rejection and failure are possibilities, but You will work all things out for my good. I want to make the first step as an ambassador for You. Show me the way and guide my steps."

WHY JESUS: DAY 7

Jesus Discovered

"Then Jesus declared, 'I am the bread of life. Whoever comes to Me will never go hungry, and whoever believes in Me will never be thirsty'" (John 6.35 NIV).

God uses many metaphors in the Bible, especially when the Bible uses descriptions for Jesus. We are physical and spiritual beings, and sometimes we need a physical representation for a spiritual truth. Jesus is called the bread of life. This bread was broken for our sins. Jesus' body was broken and hung on a cross, so that His blood, life essence of God, could pour forgiveness and grace onto the world. The entire earth has been reconciled and redeemed through Jesus' work on the cross. When we eat the bread for Eucharist, the ceremony that commemorates the Last Supper where Jesus drank the wine and broke the bread with His disciples, we remember this amazing metaphor. God left His throne, put on flesh and entered our world, so He could pour out His life-giving blood onto all of creation. The broken bread is Jesus' broken body. Jesus took our sins, carried them into the grave and rose again, leaving our sins behind. When we "break bread" with family and friends, we remember the profound sacrifice that Jesus offered on our behalf—His body.

"No one can take My life from me. I sacrifice it voluntarily. For I have the authority to lay it down when I want to and also to take it up again. For this is what My Father has commanded" (John 10.18 NLT).

Contemplative Questions

1. Do you feel like a struggle is breaking you today?

2. Can you remember a struggle from the past that you overcame and became stronger because of it?

3. How has God used your brokenness to share His glory with the people around you?

Faith Recovered

"We are hard pressed on every side, but not crushed; perplexed, but not in despair; persecuted, but not abandoned; struck down, but not destroyed" (2 Corinthians 4.8-9 NIV).

Breaking doesn't sound like a nice word. Many times we wonder why God would allow us to experience circumstances that feel like they are tearing us apart. Some trials we face are repercussions of our own sinful decisions and actions. However, other trials just happen because life isn't perfect nor fair. God allows these trials and can use all the struggles in our life to shape us into His best design. It is the hard times that cause us to rise up and change. God promises us that though we are broken, we will never be completely destroyed. Our faith becomes stronger with every hardship we overcome. We can trust that God's Spirit will be with us as He matures us in Christ.

Meditation Moment

Bitterness becomes a protection that robs us of brokenness. When we experience hardships, we may try to callous the wounds. Instead of hardening your heart, though, imagine God's soothing grace flowing through the broken areas of your life. He is healing your wounds and pouring His glory through your heartbreak.

Holy Spirit Uncovered

"Most laws condemn the soul and pronounce sentence. The result of the law of my God is perfect. It condemns but forgives. It restores – more than abundantly – what it takes away." – Jim Elliot

Jesus' body was broken so the Holy Spirit could pour out onto the world. God transformed the most detestable circumstance in history (the Son of God crucified on the cross) into the most beautiful gift of all time (the presence of the Holy Spirit). Now the Holy Spirit works on our behalf, transforming the ugly areas of our lives into precious acts of redemption. God literally can make beauty out of ashes when we give Him our brokenness (Isaiah 61.3). The world is corrupt, and we will experience trials in this life, but the Holy Spirit is constantly at work redeeming, reviving and restoring.

Professing Prayer

"Holy Spirit, I know you are showing up in my heartache. You are perpetually healing and restoring my soul. I give you my struggles because I know you can move a miracle into them. Thank You for walking through these trials with me. Life may not be fair, but I trust that I will never be alone for You are always with me."

WHY JESUS: DAY 8

Jesus Discovered

"And the LORD God made for Adam and for his wife garments of skins and clothed them" (Genesis 3.21 ESV).

When Adam and Eve were in the Garden of Eden, God gave them free will, which came in the metaphor of the Tree of Knowledge of Good and Evil. God wanted sons and daughters, not robots that had no choice to obey or disobey. He knew, though, like all children that we would make mistakes, allowing our sin to separate us from Him. So He also planted in the Garden of Eden the Tree of Life, which is Jesus Christ. Adam and Eve lost God's glory covering them, so God did the first sacrifice mentioned in the Bible. He sacrificed animals in order to cover their nakedness and shame with "garments of skin." This symbolic payment of sacrificing animals to recompense for humanity's sin is a foreshadowing in the Old Testament of what Jesus would do in the New Testament. Every time an animal was sacrificed in the Old Testament, God would see the finished work of Jesus

Christ on the cross because He lives outside of time. God rested on the seventh day of creation, or reconciliation day, knowing that Jesus would redeem all six days with His sacrifice. Starting from that first sacrifice until Jesus was led like a lamb to the slaughter, God's justice was paid (Isaiah 53.7). God is a good God who requires justice, but He is also a loving Heavenly Father who loves His children. He maintained His justice and His love through the final sacrifice offered up by Jesus Christ.

"He was oppressed and afflicted, yet He did not open His mouth; He was led like a lamb to the slaughter, and as a sheep before its shearers is silent, so He did not open His mouth" (Isaiah 53.7 NIV).

Contemplative Questions

1. Do you think justice is important? Why or why not?

2. What if God was a loving Heavenly Father but biased with His justice?

3. Jesus paid the requirement for our sin, so God could be all-loving and all righteous. How does His sacrifice change your perception of fairness?

Faith Recovered

"Beloved, have you ever thought that someday you will not have anything to try you, or to vex you again? There will be no opportunity in heaven to learn or to show the spirit of patience, forbearance, and longsuffering. If you are to practice these things, it must be now." – A.B. Simpson

Our sins do have repercussions. When we choose to disobey God, there will be amends to be made, debts to be paid and apologies to be said. However, once we receive Jesus Christ as our Lord and Savior, we will never be separated from God again. On earth, we are gifted the Holy Spirit. In heaven, we are gifted a place in the presence of God. The circumstances we face in this life are miniscule compared to enjoying an eternity with God in heaven. We don't deserve it, and we can never earn it. But it is ours for free because of Jesus' finished work on the cross.

Meditation Moment

Remember a time when you felt fully free, like a child at the lake with her family or like a son walking in victory after a game. That feeling of complete joy and love is only a shadow of what you will feel in heaven. Words can't

even describe the thick joy that will envelop us as we sit in God's presence. It is your right by the blood of Jesus Christ to sit in God's presence, allowing Him to fill you with the love, joy and peace of His holy nature.

Holy Spirit Uncovered

"Peter replied, 'Repent and be baptized, every one of you, in the name of Jesus Christ for the forgiveness of your sins. And you will receive the gift of the Holy Spirit'" (Acts 2.38 NIV).

Jesus died so He could pay for our sins and give us God's Spirit. Once we have the Holy Spirit, God sows seeds of His character inside of us. These seeds are called the Fruits of the Spirit: love, joy, peace, patience, kindness, goodness, faithfulness, gentleness, and self-control (Galatians 5.22-23). These seeds can only grow into fruit if they are planted in the tilled (humbled) soil of our souls, watered with God's Holy Word and pruned by His hand. The Holy Spirit will cultivate these seeds of God's character, so you can walk in the fullness of His bounty on earth.

Professing Prayer

"Holy Spirit, I know You have gifted me the fruits of Your Spirit. Help me to tend to these seeds, so their influence in my life can grow. I want to walk in peace and joy. I want to grow my faith, and I want to have gentleness and self-control. I desire to have large, ripe fruits of love and kindness to be a refreshing source of Your goodness to those around me."

WHY JESUS: DAY 9

Jesus Discovered

"Now if we are children, then we are heirs—heirs of God and co-heirs with Christ, if indeed we share in His sufferings in order that we may also share in His glory" (Romans 8.17 NIV).

The Passion of Christ starts at the garden of Gethsemane and ends with the death and burial of Jesus Christ. *Passion* is the Latin word meaning *to suffer*. Jesus' disciples and His other followers tried to either stop Jesus' suffering or mourned it because they did not realize the glory that was waiting for Him on the other side. When we patiently endure hardships, rejoicing in the firm belief that God can turn our trials into something beautiful, we please God and give Him life-material in which to resurrect. As co-heirs with Christ who share in Jesus' example of endurance, we will also share in His glory, producing blessings to all those around us. We may question God when suffering befalls us, but after our concern has been vented, we can trust in God's Holy

Word. We know that God is good, and He loves us. He will take our suffering and transform it into His glory. We simply need to patiently endure, and watch God resurrect beauty from our heartache.

"Of course, you get no credit for being patient if you are beaten for doing wrong. But if you suffer for doing good and endure it patiently, God is pleased with you" (1 Peter 2.20 NLT).

Contemplative Questions

1. What are you suffering today? How can you trust God with the situation?

2. What heartache from your past has God used for His glory?

3. Believing God's word over your circumstances can be difficult. What faith-resources can you consume to help you continue your belief?

Faith Recovered

"'Truly I tell you,' Jesus answered, 'this very night, before the rooster crows, you will disown Me three times'" (Matthew 26.34 NIV).

Peter wrestled with his faith. He wanted an earthly king to free his people and restore the nation of Israel. Watching Jesus take a passive role, becoming like a lamb being led to the slaughter (Isaiah 53.7), was contradictory to the expectations of those waiting for the promised Messiah, the Deliverer. Peter denied to know Jesus three times, but his story doesn't end there. It continues with the church being built upon Peter's ministry (Matthew 16.18). Peter's faith may have stumbled, but he would eventually walk in the glory that God established in him. Overcoming falls only makes our faith that much stronger.

Meditation Moment

Imagine the thing that is holding you back from achieving God's promises. What is it? Now envision it as a hurdle. It tripped you up once, twice and maybe even three times; but every time you stumble, you become stronger, wiser and more determined. Now watch yourself soar over that hurdle into the great things that God has for you.

Holy Spirit Uncovered

"Beloved, God's promises can never fail to be accomplished, and those who patiently wait can never be disappointed, for a believing faith leads to realization." – Lettie B. Cowman

Many times the reason we stumble is that we are not willing to wait. We rush ahead of God's Spirit and wonder why we can't make it over the obstacles in the way. God knows our strength. He knows when we will be ready for the burdens and the blessings of our promises. God will not open the gates to our Promised Land until His time is ready. So instead of trying to move forward only to fail, we can rest in God, lean on His word and trust the process. We won't miss our destiny. All His promises are ours through Christ, but they will not come all at once (2 Corinthians 1.20). We can focus on the blessings we have now and believe for the promises to come.

Professing Prayer

"Holy Spirit, I do not want to run ahead of You. Rather, I want to walk in sync with Your Spirit, knowing that You will prepare my way in Your perfect timing. Help me to appreciate all that You have blessed me with now. I don't

Alisa Hope Wagner
WHY JESUS

want to waste one more moment longing for something for which I am not ready."

Why Jesus: Day 10

Jesus Discovered

"I saw heaven standing open and there before me was a white horse, whose rider is called Faithful and True..." (Revelation 19.11 NIV).

The writer of Revelation through the inspiration of the Holy Spirit calls Jesus faithful and true. Regardless of what we experience in this broken world, and regardless of what our intellect and feelings tell us, Jesus Christ is faithful and true. *Faithful* means loyal, steadfast and unwavering. Jesus can always be counted on. He will always have our best interest at heart. He will never leave us nor forsake us. *True* means to be accurate, right and factual. Jesus is not a fairytale, and He's not simply a metaphor of a higher being. Yes, there are many metaphors to describe Him (shepherd, door, way, light, bread, etc.), but He Himself actually walked this earth. He lived and breathed and died, like all of us will do. To know that our God can identify with us so completely through the Person of Jesus Christ offers us hope that we can live out this life of faith on earth. When hardships come our way, we must always remember that Jesus is unwavering in His love and loyalty to us, and that everything God says about Jesus in His Holy Word can be counted on.

"Keep your lives free from the love of money and be content with what you have, because God has said, 'Never will I leave you; never will I forsake you'" (Hebrews 13.5 NIV).

Contemplative Questions

1. Do you have circumstances in your life that seem to contradict what you know about Jesus?

2. We live in a fallen world, but Jesus is continually faithful. How has He been faithful during the hard times?

3. Jesus and what He says in the Bible are always true. What are some of His promises that can affirm His goodness?

Faith Recovered

"For I am convinced that neither death nor life, neither angels nor demons, neither the present nor the future, nor any powers, neither height nor depth, nor anything else in all creation, will be able to separate us from the love of God that is in Christ Jesus our Lord" (Romans 8.38-39 NIV).

Paul went through some pretty hard times during his missionary trips as he spread the Good News of Jesus Christ. But no matter what, he clung onto what he knew. God loved him, and Jesus Christ reconciled him back to a perfect Father. This life is difficult, and we will face many trials. We may even come to the point when we wonder why we even bother with living. But compared to eternity, the struggles in this life are fleeting. God's love for us should always be the motivation that keeps us going every day. He loves us. He is for us. He wants us to live a life that honors Him. There is nothing so dark that could possibly shut out the light of God's love in our hearts, minds, souls and lives.

Meditation Moment

There are oppressive, dark circumstances all around you, trying to fill you with the chill of desperation, defeat and loneliness. However, you have the Holy Spirit inside of you through the work of Jesus on the cross. The Holy Spirit has the oil of God's love pouring out from within you. Imagine God's love warming you from the inside out, protecting you in dark circumstances.

Holy Spirit Uncovered

"Whatever is stealing your peace and rocking your boat, whatever is taking your smile away, reach down, pick it up, and throw it overboard." – Jentezen Franklin

Jesus said that He would give us peace, so we don't have to be worried or afraid during hard times (John 14.27). This peace is found in the Holy Spirit who resides in each person who accepts Jesus as Lord and Savior. The seed of peace must be watered by the Holy Spirit to grow ripe, so we may enjoy its sweetness. Communing with the Holy Spirit each day will allow Him access to fill us with His peace. The more we feel the ache of circumstances surrounding us, the more we press into God's Spirit. When we are agitated, we pray. When we are distressed, we read His Holy Word. When our heart shudders within us, we cling onto His promises. Nothing in this world can give us peace free of negative effects other than God's Spirit in us.

Professing Prayer

"Holy Spirit, I don't want to turn to other quick-fixes to help me during this dark time. I know that You are faithful and true, and that knowledge gives me peace. I am not alone—for You are with me every step of the way. Come into my situation, and create in me a peace that surpasses all understanding."

WHY JESUS: DAY 11

Jesus Discovered

"For what man knows the things of a man except the spirit of the man which is in him? Even so no one knows the things of God except the Spirit of God" (1 Corinthians 2.11 NKJV).

No one can possibly fathom the amazing things that God has in store for His people—both in this temporal life and our eternal life. However, as Christians, we don't have to make limited speculations. Because of Jesus' work on the cross, we now have the Holy Spirit residing inside of us. We have been supernaturally made holy by the blood of Jesus Christ, so God's Spirit can establish His home—heaven—in our hearts. We can now ask God to reveal His plans to us. He may not give us the entire view, but He can certainly give us a portion of the picture each day. We have received God's Spirit, so we don't have to trust the corrupted spirit of this world and its thought-processes and belief-systems. We can experience this life through eternal eyes, shaping our beliefs, thoughts, words and actions with a higher view. We have what the world does not have—access to God's vantage point anytime. We simply need to sit in His presence, read His Holy Word and listen to His voice.

"For since the world began, no ear has heard and no eye has seen a God like You, Who works for those who wait for Him!" (Isaiah 64.4 NLT).

Contemplative Questions

1. Have you cultivated a lifestyle of leaning on God to guide you?

2. Is there an instance in your life where God showed you something or had you do something to prepare you for a future event?

3. Sometimes following God's will can seem confusing, but we will eventually realize how much time and energy we save trusting Him. What is an area of your life that you have not fully given to His care and guidance?

Faith Recovered

"God has guarded His Word so that only the pure in heart can see its secrets. All other efforts will fail." – Winkie Pratney

The Bible is full of God's unfathomable truths. And God wants to share so much with us. However, He will not give us revelatory understanding and knowledge if our motives are wrong. Selfish gain and self-glory can come in many forms—even masquerading as something that seems good to the outside world. When we read God's Holy Word, our hearts should want to know God more and to make Him known to the world. Critical eyes will only find fuel in the verses to judge and condemn others. But those with a pure heart will use their understanding to set captives free (Luke 4.18). We can expect God to speak to us today through His Holy Word. He longs to share His truth with us, so we can be a light of His love and grace to others.

Meditation Moment

When you open the Bible today, ask God to give you revelation knowledge that will encourage and free not only yourself but the people in your life. Pray before you read His Holy Word, asking Him to make Himself known

to you. Imagine the Holy Spirit sitting next to you, guiding you through every verse.

Holy Spirit Uncovered

"Ask me and I will tell you remarkable secrets you do not know about things to come" (Jeremiah 33.3 NLT).

Secrets are usually told between intimate friends. People who value their purpose and life will not simply share their greatest secrets with just anyone. We want to trust those to whom we reveal our very souls to. The Holy Spirit is no different. He wants to share His secrets with us, so He must trust us with the knowledge. Then He will create a curriculum with us, so we can study His Holy Word with Him. The Bible is the only book in all of history that has never-ending depth and meaning. We can read the Bible over and over again for our entire lives and not receive the fullness of its knowledge. We can start today, reading the Bible every day. The Holy Spirit will supply us with everything we need to be victorious in our daily lives.

Professing Prayer

"Holy Spirit, I want to read the Bible with You. Will You be my reading partner and reveal God's secrets to me, so I can be prepared with all the wisdom, understanding and knowledge to live my life in victory and abundance. Make sure my heart is pure. I want to use my insight to love others and show them Jesus."

WHY JESUS: DAY 12

Jesus Discovered

"For no matter how many promises God has made, they are 'Yes' in Christ. And so through Him the 'Amen' is spoken by us to the glory of God" (2 Corinthians 1.20 NIV).

Although we all fall short of God's glory, we are redeemed through Jesus Christ. Without Jesus, nothing we do can be pleasing to God. Jesus reconciles all of our actions done in obedience to God and erases all of our actions done in disobedience to sin. Even when our intentions are pure and we are faithful to God's will, we will never in our own strength please God and deserve His abundant blessings. We achieve God's promises simply by believing Him at His word and acting in that belief, knowing that Jesus' finished work on the cross makes all of our efforts perfect in God's eyes. That is why our promises are sure in Christ alone. Nothing we can do or say can ever be good enough to earn God's favor and grace, but we are imparted God's best because of His great love for us—a love demonstrated through the life, death and resurrection of Jesus Christ. So when God gives us a promise that we do not deserve, we can say "amen," trusting that Jesus has fulfilled all the requirements on our behalf. We only need to claim those promises by faith and display that faith in our words, attitudes and actions!

"Therefore, I tell you, whatever you ask for in prayer, believe that you have received it, and it will be yours" (Mark 11.24 NIV).

Contemplative Questions

1. Has God given you crazy, big promises? What are a few?

2. Do you find it difficult to believe in those promises? Why or why not?

3. God cannot contradict His promises in your life. How can you make actions of faith toward your promises today?

Faith Recovered

"Yet he did not waver through unbelief regarding the promise of God, but was strengthened in his faith and gave glory to God, being fully persuaded that God had power to do what He had promised" (Romans 4.20-21 NIV).

God promised Abraham that he would have a child with Sarah. However, old age would say otherwise. Yet, Abraham held onto God's promise by supernatural faith rather than natural sight (2 Corinthians 5.7). And it was credited to him as righteousness not because Abraham was perfect, but because he was faithful. Having faith against all odds in the promises that God has given us will be the one struggle we all must overcome and claim victory over. God is outside of time, and He sees our promises being fulfilled, but we must choose to trust Him over our lack. Unbelief will try to dig its jagged claws into us and suck out all of our faith, but we can stand firm in our faith despite what all the natural circumstances surrounding us declare.

Meditation Moment

Imagine God's promises already in your reach. Find a photo that captures your promises and carry it with you.

Alisa Hope Wagner
WHY JESUS

Write a declaration of belief and repeat it every day. Imagine yourself walking in your Promised Land whenever your faith wavers. Do whatever it takes to keep your faith in God's promises alive.

Holy Spirit Uncovered

"I believe the promises of God enough to venture an eternity on them." – Isaac Watts

Many Christians will believe in God's promise to save them by the blood of Jesus, but they won't believe in God's simpler promises of destiny. The mere fact that we are able to have a relationship with a Holy God even in our sinful state and one day will be in His glory in heaven is the miracle of all miracles. Every other promise is relatively small compared to the eternity of our souls. If we are resting our eternal souls on faith in God's promises, it should be easy to rest our earthly promises on faith in His promises. Living by faith is the life of every Believer. We get into trouble when we rely more on our physical sight and our own strength. There comes a time in all our lives that we open our arms and take a leap of faith into our destiny, trusting that the Holy Spirit will help us soar.

Professing Prayer

"Holy Spirit, I want to trust God's promises even though they seem impossible or even silly. I know that You are with me, willing me to make a move by faith and guiding me in steps of belief. I'm shutting my eyes today and giving You permission to lead me. The way seems dark to me, but I know that You see and know all."

Why Jesus: Day 13

Jesus Discovered

"For we do not have a high priest who cannot sympathize with our weaknesses, but One who has been tempted in all things as we are, yet without sin" (Hebrews 4.15 NASB).

Jesus truly understands us because He has experienced the sin of the world. He took all of humanity's sin, illness, pain and weakness, exchanging it for His holiness and perfection. We don't have to fear our God not understanding us. The Bible says Jesus "has been tempted in all things as we are." We can come to Jesus in prayer with our struggles and temptations, knowing that He has already overcome every trouble that the world throws our way. Even though we are weak, He is strong. We must claim defeat in our own strength, relying solely on the resurrection power of Jesus Christ in our lives. Jesus has already overcome our every battle. We simply need to rejoice in our victory by faith. It's not about what we need to do. It's about what Jesus has already done for us. We can walk victoriously in each area of our lives because the grace of Jesus Christ extends to the places and situations where we have need.

"I have told you these things, so that in Me you may have peace. In this world you will have trouble. But take heart! I have overcome the world" (John 16.33 NIV).

Contemplative Questions

1. Are you struggling with something that you think Jesus either can't handle or doesn't care about?

2. What temptations should you avoid because you don't have the strength to overcome them?

3. Jesus only wants to correct you, not condemn you. Will you open yourself up to His correcting hand, so he can restore, heal and protect you?

Faith Recovered

"The essence of temptation is the invitation to live independently of God." – Neil T. Anderson

When we stop relying on God, we take ourselves out from under God's shade of protection. God is moving in the perfect pattern for our best life, and we must lean on Him every day in order to stay aligned with His will and under His protection. When we stop relying on Him, we will begin to go places we don't have the grace for and do things that will leave us exhausted. No matter how good our actions look on the outside, if they are not submitted to the Holy Spirit, we will never have His abundance and ease in that area. Temptation begins when we stop seeking God. An easy way to guard against temptation is to go to Him every day – even when we feel rushed or we feel we don't need to spend that time with Him. Making God our lifestyle will ensure that we stay in the peace and prosperity of His protection.

Meditation Moment

Imagine that God's best way is like railroad tracks lining the length of your life. You might have enough fuel to leave those tracks for a while, but eventually you'll get lost and run out of power. If you get rooted to Him every

day, His unceasing energy will take you everywhere you need to go with unlimited peace and stamina. Make sure to connect with Him each day, but if you get off track, go quickly back to the source.

Holy Spirit Uncovered

"We all, like sheep, have gone astray, each of us has turned to our own way; and the LORD has laid on Him the iniquity of us all" (Isaiah 53.6 NIV).

People like to categorize sin from least to greatest, but the ultimate sin is our desire to walk our own way, which is pride. Pride prevents us from coming to God and submitting to Him. The truth is, though, that we are nothing without God. He created us and gives us His value and purpose. If we knew the great and wonderful things that He had in store for us, we would realize that our meager offerings look like nothing compared to His. God gives us His Spirit in our imperfect state and in a corrupt world. This is the mystery of grace. This is the undeserved gift of friendship with God. The Holy Spirit came at a high price – the death of Jesus – and walking away from such a prize is a travesty. Let us not think ourselves higher than God. Let us listen and obey the Holy Spirit. His ways are always perfect.

Professing Prayer

"Holy Spirit, I know how easy it is to go my own way. I understand that it starts with little compromises until I finally see how much off track I've gotten. Expose areas in my life that are not submitted to You. Let me quickly repent and bring those areas back under your authority."

Why Jesus: Day 14

Jesus Discovered

"About three in the afternoon Jesus cried out in a loud voice, 'Eli, Eli, *lema sabachthani*?' (which means 'My God, my God, why have you forsaken me?')" (Matthew 27.46 NIV).

Jesus took our forsakenness, so we would never be forsaken. When Jesus hung on the cross, it wasn't the pain that made Him cry out. It wasn't our sin He took that caused Him to petition God. It was the separation He felt from God. All Jesus had ever known was connectivity to God. But as He took the sins of the world on His shoulders, He felt God look away because God can have no part of sin. And for that short time, Jesus called out to His Father, feeling the physical and spiritual death upon Him, asking: "My God, my God, why have you forsaken me?" Because of Jesus' finished work on the cross, those are words that we will never have to utter. Regardless of what happens in this life, if we have Jesus in our hearts, God will never leave nor forsake us. Jesus took our separation from God and gave us His connectivity to God, so that in this life and in the next life we can dwell in the presence of our Heavenly Father. Jesus filled the gaping hole that divided us from God with Himself. He took our forsakenness, bridged the gap that sin created and drew all of the earth to Himself, resurrecting us into new lives with Him.

"Let your conduct be without covetousness; be content with such things as you have. For He Himself has said, 'I will never leave you nor forsake you'" (Hebrews 13.5 NKJV).

Contemplative Questions

1. How does knowing that you will never be forsaken help you to face life's trials?

2. Connectivity to God came at a high price. What ways can you personally cultivate your relationship with God?

3. Who else can you tell about Jesus' gift of salvation?

Faith Recovered

"Though justification costs us nothing but the sacrifice of our pride, it has cost Christ His blood." – F.B. Meyer

The gift of salvation costs us absolutely nothing, yet it costs Jesus everything. Jesus left His throne, He clothed Himself in flesh and entered our corrupt world. Then He lived a perfect life and died, so we could be reconciled back to God. He took our sin into the tomb and left it there, resurrecting Himself on the third day. He gave us God's Holy Spirit and ascended back to the Father in heaven. This is a free gift to us and to everyone. It is simple and easy to share. It may feel weird or difficult sharing the Gospel with other people, but a gift so priceless must be offered. Not only do we share the Gospel with our words, we share it with our lives. Once we let go of our pride and humble ourselves to God, there is no telling how He can use us to expand His kingdom and reach His people.

Meditation Moment

God has placed you precisely in this time and on this earth to be a spokesperson for His love. Sharing Jesus doesn't have to be difficult. If we don't have the words just yet, we can share a book, song, sermon or article that does.

Start sharing Him with the people who God has placed in your life.

Holy Spirit Uncovered

"When they take you to the places of worship and to the courts and to the leaders of the country, do not be worried about what you should say or how to say it. The Holy Spirit will tell you what you should say at that time" (Luke 12.11-12 NLV).

We don't have to worry about what we will say when we share Jesus with others. If we are praying and studying the Bible, the Holy Spirit will give us exactly the words to say. The Holy Spirit will use the treasures that we have stored in our heart to create a testimony of His love from our lips to our audience's ears. We can be aggressive about reading and meditating on God's Holy Word, knowing that He will eventually use the insights we are gleaning and storing up. He might not use them today or tomorrow, but one day those words of knowledge will be plucked by the Holy Spirit and offered to someone who desperately needs to hear them.

Professing Prayer

"Holy Spirit, I want to be aggressive about studying God's Holy Word and praying to You, so I can have a heart filled with revelatory knowledge and understanding. Forgive me for taking my Bible and other biblical resources for granted. Help me to make time to study Your Holy Word and to listen to Your voice."

WHY JESUS: DAY 15

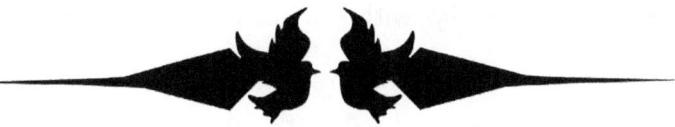

Jesus Discovered

"Truly, God will not do wrong. The Almighty will not twist justice" (Job 34.12 NLT).

People wonder why the cross is important. If God is God, why can't He just forgive our sins without payment? Why did Jesus need to sacrifice His perfect life on the cross to pay for our guilt-debt? The answer is simple: God is a just God. Yes, He is Love, but He is also justice. He will not "twist justice." He cannot be corrupted even by His great love for His children. He could not govern heaven and earth if He compromised His own standard. So instead of allowing us to die in our guilt, which we deserve, He paid for our guilt through the death and resurrection of Jesus Christ. Therefore, both God's love and His justice stand arm in arm, neither compromised or removed, standing as pillars, upholding God's great universe. Only a sinless person could take the guilt of another person. Otherwise, he would still have his own guilt to pay and unable to pay for the guilt of another. But Jesus was guiltless, and He gave us His perfection in exchange for our shame. He buried our sin in the grave and rose again leaving that sin behind. We have been made righteous, holy and perfect by the finished work of Jesus on the cross, so now we can have a relationship with our loving and just Heavenly Father.

"Could God govern if he hated justice? Are you going to condemn the almighty judge?" (Job 34.17).

Contemplative Questions

1. If love could sway a judge to overlook the standards of the law, would that judge be just?

2. God is able to fully love us because Jesus Christ took our sin. How does this Good News change the way you view the cross?

3. Now that you have freedom from sin, what changes can you make to walk in that freedom?

Faith Recovered

"There are two freedoms - the false, where a man is free to do what he likes; the true, where he is free to do what he ought." – Charles Finney

The grace of God extended to us through the finished work of Jesus Christ gives us freedom not to indulge in our own desires but to commit ourselves to the desires of God. Many people do and will abuse grace. They know they are saved by grace, and they take their salvation through Jesus and neglect their relationship with Him. Just like an empty marriage, a husband and a wife can be married by law yet be strangers in their own home. We can have salvation and lack relationship. Grace forgives us of our sin, but it also enables us to fulfill our destiny. Jesus' blood erases our sin and gives us a clean slate to establish God's glory in our lives and the world around us. However, many people who have neglected fellowshipping with God, will go to eternity and have nothing to show for their lives because they walked in salvation but not relationship.

Meditation Moment

Imagine your life as a book. All the sin has been erased by the blood of Jesus Christ, but your fellowship with God

and your obedience to His Word will fill the pages of this book with faith-works and Christ-like character. Now envision giving this book to Jesus once you are face-to-face with Him in heaven. Will He be pleased or disappointed with what you did with your freedom in Him?

Holy Spirit Uncovered

"So if the Son makes you free, you will be free for sure" (John 8.36 NLV).

Freedom in Christ means that we are no longer bound by sin. Now we have the Holy Spirit in our hearts, guiding, encouraging, convicting and empowering us to achieve God's will. God has great plans for us – and these plans will transform our lives into bestselling heavenly books. The Holy Spirit knows how to put God's best words on the pages of our time. The sin and mistakes are continually being erased, and God is weaving our sorrow and joy into His Great Kingdom Story. We have freedom to follow God with all of our hearts, knowing that the Master Writer is creating a plot of love, redemption and victory with our every step. We don't have to fear our freedom if we simply have faith.

Professing Prayer

"Holy Spirit, I want You to write me into the most exciting plot of all time! I want to obey You and trust that You know what You are doing. You have great plans for me. Now that I'm no longer trapped by sin, I can walk in the freedom of the purposes You have written on the pages of my life."

WHY JESUS: DAY 16

Jesus Discovered

"Then the LORD God planted a garden in Eden in the east, and there He placed the man He had made" (Genesis 2.8 NLT).

Heaven is the presence of God. Hell is the absence of God. People can give human descriptions of heaven, using our five senses, but really heaven is more than a place, it is a presence. God is the embodiment of all that is good, so heaven is the extension of this goodness around all of creation. The first heaven in which humans lived was Eden, the garden of God. However, we used our free will to sin, and because of that sin, God's glory around us was replaced with our shame. We could no longer stay in God's presence, His heavenly garden, anymore. God knew His children would fall from grace, so His redemption plan through Jesus Christ was already in place. It was a tree that caused us to sin, so it would be a tree that Jesus would hang on to pay for our sin. It took the glory of the Tree of Life (Jesus) to replace the shame caused by the Tree of Knowledge. Because of the finished work of Jesus Christ, we have heaven, or the presence of God, inside of us. Our shame is lifted, and we have God's glory around us once again.

"The God of our fathers raised Jesus, Whom you killed by hanging Him on a tree" (Acts 5.30 ESV).

Contemplative Questions

1. God knew we would sin, but He always has a plan of redemption. How has God redeemed your life?

2. Redemption of past mistakes can be missed in certain areas if we don't obey God's leading. What is God wanting you to do today, so that His redemption plan can be established?

3. How does knowing no one is perfect besides Jesus help you to offer forgiveness more freely to yourself and others?

Faith Recovered

"It flowed down the center of the main street. On each side of the river grew a tree of life, bearing twelve crops of fruit, with a fresh crop each month. The leaves were used for medicine to heal the nations" (Revelation 22.2 NLT).

The tree represents God's blessings and fullness in our lives. These blessings are encased in a promise or vision that He buries deep within our spirit. In the Bible, there are three significant trees: the Tree of Life in Genesis 2.9, the Tree of Death (the cross) and the Tree of Life in Revelation. The Tree of Life in Revelation is the Resurrected Tree of Life in Genesis. In between the Genesis Tree and the Revelation Tree is the Tree of Death (the cross). Jesus' death on the cross is the doorway to pass from the unattainable Genesis Tree to the attainable Revelation Tree. All things must pass through the middle tree, dying in the natural to be resurrected in the supernatural. God gives us a vision for our life. This vision is perfect like the Genesis Tree. However, we sin and we fall short. The vision becomes unattainable, so it must die on the cross in order for Jesus to resurrect it. Only then does our vision become attainable like the Revelation Tree.

Meditation Moment

God has given you a promise for your life. What is it? Imagine it as the Tree of Genesis. It is just out of your reach. Now envision that promise dying on the cross. You must let go, so Jesus can resurrect it. Stop trying to achieve your dreams alone. Give them to God. Let them die in the natural, so they can be resurrected in the supernatural. Now imagine your promise as the Revelation Tree, blessing you and the people around you.

Holy Spirit Uncovered

"Jesus took the tree of death so you could have the tree of life." – Tim Keller

Jesus took our death, so we could have life in Him. This is what we call redemption. Part of the redeemed life is the free gift of the Holy Spirit within us while we live on this earth. One day, when we are in heaven, we will experience the Holy Spirit (God's Spirit) with all of our senses. He will light up all of eternity with His presence, and we won't have to perceive Him by faith. But until then, we must cultivate our relationship with Him by faith and belief in what the Bible says to be true. Jesus' finished work on the cross is the doorway to not only our salvation and fellowship with God, but it is also the key to our full purpose. And the system of redemption is the same: We have an unattainable promise which must die and be resurrected in Christ. Our life, our dreams, our desires all must die within the belly of Jesus and the tomb, so the power and the abundance of the Holy Spirit can pour over all we have and do.

Professing Prayer

"Holy Spirit, pour all over me and my life. I give up control and allow Jesus to do His resurrecting work in all I say, do and create. I see now that the dreams that God has given me are unattainable without the resurrecting work of Jesus Christ in them. Create in me a Tree of Life that is attainable through the grace of Jesus. Fill my work with Your satisfying and healing fruit."

WHY JESUS: DAY 17

Jesus Discovered

"God sent His Son into the world not to judge the world, but to save the world through Him. There is no judgment against anyone who believes in Him. But anyone who does not believe in Him has already been judged for not believing in God's One and only Son" (John 3.17-18 NLT).

Hell is the absence of God. God does not send us to hell; rather, we choose to walk in the absence of God when we don't accept Jesus Christ as our Savior. We can only be in the presence of God if we are perfect and holy as God is perfect and holy. But we can't in our own strength or through our own diligence ever be perfect and holy. We must have a mediator to extend this holiness and perfection to us. Once we accept Jesus Christ as our Lord and Savior, we can have a relationship with God. That relationship continues after we die and we enter into heaven. If we don't have a relationship with God through the finished work of Jesus Christ on the cross, that lack of relationship we have with God on earth will continue. We will be separated from God because we lack a relationship with Him that's only possible through a Messiah, Jesus Christ. This is hell, and God does not want even one of His children to go there.

"They will be punished with eternal destruction, forever separated from the Lord and from His glorious power" (2 Thessalonians 1.9 NLT).

Contemplative Questions

1. In Christ, we are able to have a relationship with God. What would your life be like today if you had never given your life over to Jesus?

2. Everyone has a testimony—stories of God's goodness and redemption in their lives. What is one story that you could share with others?

3. The truth that Jesus rescued us from eternal separation from God is the highest Good News in all of creation. Can you praise Jesus today and let Him know how thankful you are?

Faith Recovered

"And being found in appearance as a man, He humbled Himself by becoming obedient to death—even death on a cross!" (Philippians 2.8 NIV).

Being found in God is just the beginning of our walk of faith. We come to God much like a baby: needy, weak and immature. However, God does not want to leave us in that condition. This life is much like a womb. God allows resistance to come against us because that is how we grow and mature. We are naturally minded when we first come to God, and peeling the layers of our selfish nature takes time. The process is not always fun, and sometimes it even hurts. But learning to trust and rely on God shapes us into the image of Christ who was obedient even unto death. Faith sometimes can feel like a burden if we don't fully believe that God has our best interest at heart. God loves us and we are literally His children through Jesus Christ. He loves us so much that He desires us to become the people He created us to be.

Meditation Moment

Understanding that God's love is what allows resistance to come against you feels like a paradox. If someone loves you, why would he or she allow you to experience hard times? But most parents, teachers and other authority figures realize that those in our care will never rise to maturity if everything is quick and easy. Take account of the resistance coming against you today and allow it to force you to rise up and grow in Christ.

Holy Spirit Uncovered

"We will also do well to understand that anything which comes to us easily or quickly is usually insignificant." – Rick Joyner

Nothing truly valuable and eternal comes quickly or easily, besides salvation in Christ, which is a free gift. Everything else, however, must be cultivated with faith and belief against obstacles of all kinds. The dying of self—our desires, our judgments, our plans—gives way to the fullness of the Holy Spirit in all we do. We can't just have perseverance, we must have a childlike reliance on God. Although God is maturing us spiritually, our trust in Him should always be like that of a trusting child who depends on his or her father. We can become jaded after facing many obstacles and not seeing God's promises come to fruition, but we must trust that God has a plan. All His promises are sure. God cannot go against His word. God will complete what He started in us, but it won't be quick or easy. The distance we run with God teaches us to find rest in Him.

Professing Prayer

"Holy Spirit, I'm feeling so weary today. I've overcome so many obstacles and have allowed God-ordained resistance to mature and grow me. But after rising up time and time again, I still haven't experienced Your Spirit flooding my situation. I want to have childlike faith—always feeling secure that You are true to Your word. Let me find rest in You. I choose not to give up, and I'm ready for the next phase of our journey together."

WHY JESUS: DAY 18

Jesus Discovered

"The LORD God made all kinds of trees grow out of the ground—trees that were pleasing to the eye and good for food. In the middle of the garden were the tree of life and the tree of the knowledge of good and evil" (Genesis 2.9 NLT).

There were two trees in the Garden of Eden—one representing our free will and the other representing the redemption of our free will. The Tree of Knowledge of Good and Evil allows us the right to make our own choices in obedience or disobedience to God. And the Tree of Life is Jesus Christ who hung on a tree to save us from the fallout of our choices done outside of God's will. Jesus' blood erases the bad that we create and His light shines on the good we create. He wants us to be creators as He Himself is a Creator. He designed us in His very own image, so we can create beauty for His glory. But that freedom came at a cost. Because of our choices that are done outside of God's will, we now know good and evil.

Good is everything inside God and evil is everything outside of God. God did not create evil, but because good exists, the absence of good also exists. But praise be to God, we can create good for God's glory while Jesus offers us continual mercy and forgiveness for our flaws and mistakes.

"If we confess our sins, He is faithful and just and will forgive us our sins and purify us from all unrighteousness" (1 John 1.9 NIV).

Contemplative Questions

1. What free will choices have you made that created destruction or chaos in your life? How did God redeem your actions once you repented to Him?

2. What free will choices have you made that created beauty and peace in your life? How did God shine His grace on your actions?

3. Free will came at the price of Jesus. What can you create today that will give Him glory?

Faith Recovered

"At least there is hope for a tree: If it is cut down, it will sprout again, and its new shoots will not fail" (Job 14.7 NIV).

Sometimes it feels like God has completely chopped off everything we have ever known. He has either allowed everything to be taken away from us or He has asked us to walk away from everything by faith. Both situations can leave us feeling lost and alone. We must trust, though, that God would not take something away without replacing it with something better. Job from the Bible knew all too well how it felt to lose everything, and he wrestled with his faith. But when he finally realized that God's ways are always sovereign, he submitted to the process. Then God allowed new "shoots" to grow in the empty space that had been made in Job's life. God sees things through a heavenly, eternal perspective which may confuse us because we are limited to space and time. We can trust that when God creates space in our lives by removing things, He will fill that emptiness with the new growth of His abundance and favor.

Meditation Moment

Imagine the emptiness in your life that has been created either by loss or obedience. The tree of your life has been chopped short and those branches you held near are now gone. Allow God to grow newness in the void. Give Him your pain, so He can replace your heartache with His goodness and grace.

Holy Spirit Uncovered

"That person is like a tree planted by streams of water, which yields its fruit in season and whose leaf does not wither—whatever they do prospers" (Psalm 1.3 NIV).

The Bible compares us to trees. If we want to bear much fruit—having evidence of God's presence in our lives—we must be planted by the streams of water. The three streams leading from God to us include reading the Bible, praying to God and obeying His Spirit. These three actions unleash the waters of God into our lives, saturating our beliefs, thoughts, words and actions with His majesty. The more we read, pray and obey, the more fruit God can produce in us. This fruit not only nourishes us, it can nourish the people around us with God's goodness. When the waters feel like they are running dry, it's time to press into the streams and allow more flow into our hearts, minds and spirits.

Professing Prayer

"Holy Spirit, I know that the well of your goodness never runs dry. If I am feeling thirsty for You, I can open Your Holy Word and drink from Scripture. I can sit at the foot of Your throne and dive into Your presence. Or I can listen for Your voice and obey what I've been putting off or ignoring. Teach me how to grow my roots into Your streams, so I can be like a tree with fruit in every season."

WHY JESUS: DAY 19

Jesus Discovered

"Do not think that I have come to abolish the Law or the Prophets; I have not come to abolish them but to fulfill them" (Matthew 5.17 NIV).

As the Bible chronicles Jesus' ministry on earth, it becomes increasingly clear that He does not obey all of the commands of Moses that are supposed to keep the Jewish people holy. He touches dead people, doesn't always wash His hands before eating, performs miracles on Sabbath, etc. In all these incidences, Jesus allows His love to usurp the Law, and many of the Pharisees call Him on it. But what the religious leaders did not recognize is that Jesus fulfilled the Law, so God's love could pour out. The Law has been fulfilled through the death and resurrection of Jesus Christ on the cross, and now we are free to love others with God's heavenly compassion. We have been made holy and blameless in God's eyes, and we are now God's righteousness through Jesus Christ (2 Corinthians 5.21). There is no more struggling to be holy because God's grace has completely fulfilled the law. He no longer has to choose between justice and love, because justice has been achieved through Jesus' sacrifice on the cross. The love of our Heavenly Father can now push to all the four corners of the earth without compromising His holiness. Because Jesus fulfilled the Law, the greatest commandment to love God and others is easier than ever.

"Jesus replied: 'Love the Lord your God with all your heart and with all your soul and with all your mind.' This is the first and greatest commandment. And the second is like it: 'Love your neighbor as yourself.' All the Law and the Prophets hang on these two commandments" (Matthew 22.37-38 NIV).

Contemplative Questions

1. Was there ever a time that you did something you thought you would never do in order to show God's love to someone?

2. Have you ever ventured into the darkness of this world in hopes of bringing someone you love to light through Jesus Christ?

3. Loving others can be messy and difficult, but staying clean and safe is not the answer. How can you show love without allowing the world to drag you down?

Faith Recovered

"For truly I tell you, until heaven and earth disappear, not the smallest letter, not the least stroke of a pen, will by any means disappear from the Law until everything is accomplished" (Matthew 5.18 NIV).

Sometimes God's love asks us to go into the darkness of this world where His beloved lost children are. Jesus came into our corrupted world, died on the cross and became sin because of His great love for us. However, sometimes Christians—because of fear, insecurity or selfishness—are not willing to go where the people are. We stay safe in our clean churches and homes and wonder why we are not having a bigger impact on the world. The lost people are out there, living in their personal, godless worlds. They crave a Creator although they may not realize it or even deny it. It is up to us to venture to them and share the love of Jesus Christ with them. It will be messy because people are messy, but because of Jesus' finished work on the cross, God will be with us every step of the way. We can ask for His love to permeate within us, so we can take risks to reach those who need Him.

Meditation Moment

Think of the person or ministry that came to you with the Good News of Jesus Christ. What condition were you in? Were you lost and hopeless, wondering about the meaning of life and your purpose on the earth? Thank God that there were people who loved enough to step outside of their comfort zones to bring you out of darkness and into the light.

Holy Spirit Uncovered

"Though we cannot think alike, may we not love alike? May we not be of one heart, though we are not of one opinion? Without all doubt, we may. Herein all the children of God may unite, notwithstanding these smaller differences." – John Wesley

One of the biggest obstacles people must overcome when reaching others for Christ is differences. Each person is unique with a one-of-a-kind background, design, purpose and viewpoint. We can let these differences separate us or be the springboard for choosing love over all else. God has called us to be one body in Christ. We are each different because we each have individual roles to play and needs to fill. When we get sidetracked by these differences, our effectiveness in the world will decrease. However, if we learn to look beyond the differences and allow love to be the oil that makes all run smoothly, we will greatly change the world. Only when we stop fighting and start working together will we stand united as a loving force in the world.

Professing Prayer

"Holy Spirit, I know that there are a lot of people who disagree with me and I may disagree with them on certain issues. But these issues pale in comparison to the main truth of Jesus Christ. If we can agree that Jesus is the Savior that the world desperately needs, then we can accomplish anything in His name."

WHY JESUS: DAY 20

Jesus Discovered

"So He sent two of His disciples, telling them, 'Go into the city, and a man carrying a jar of water will meet you. Follow him'" (Mark 14.13 NIV).

Jesus sent two of His disciples to find a man in the city who happened to be carrying a jar of water. This man would lead the disciples to an upper room that was set for Passover, yet it did not have any Passover participants. Passover is the Jewish holiday that started in Egypt when God's people were slaves, and the spirit of death passed over the homes that had the lamb's blood on the doorposts (Exodus 12.13). The fact that this upper room was set for the holiday without guests shows a lot of faith. Many times, God has us prepare for a moment that we cannot foresee. We get the upper room of our destiny ready, but we don't know exactly when Jesus is going to show up and fill our prepared emptiness with His presence. We can remain faithful and carry the "jug of water" or the presence of the Holy Spirit with us wherever we go, trusting that God will find us faithful to our calling. We must trust that He will show up exactly at the right time, but we need to be ready by faith, and believe that He will occupy the work and preparation we diligently created in our lives for Him. We may never know exactly when Jesus will show up into our destiny, but we can cling tightly to His promises.

"But about that day or hour no one knows, not even the angels in heaven, nor the Son, but only the Father. As it was in the days of Noah, so it will be at the coming of the Son of Man" (Matthew 24.36-37 NIV).

Contemplative Questions

1. Has God called you to a work that feels empty and useless? Are you believing and waiting for Jesus to suddenly show up in your readiness?

2. Working by faith is one of the most difficult actions to take because there may not be evidence of fruitfulness in the natural. Can you make a choice to put your faith above sight?

3. When Jesus does show up in your obedience, what is one thing you will do to celebrate?

Faith Recovered

"Trying to do the Lord's work in your own strength is the most confusing, exhausting, and tedious of all work. But when you are filled with the Holy Spirit, then the ministry of Jesus just flows out of you." – Corrie Ten Boom

The world has a bottom line, but God has an eternal perspective that is much different than our own. What looks unproductive to the world may very well be the highest calling in God's eyes. We can't judge our work by what the world says because the world is run by a distorted spirit that is not of God. The most valuable work is of a servant, which the world deems as lowly. Jesus came to serve, and He is Lord of Lords and King of Kings. When we feel like our work is worthless, we may have to gain a higher vantage point. Jesus will enter our faithfulness when the time is right. God's Spirit loves to dwell in a humble heart, so He can shine His glory to the world.

Meditation Moment

Make an inventory of all your work. List what you do from greatest to least according to what the world says. Once you are done, envision the list of work being reversed. What you put last is really first, and what you put first is

Alisa Hope Wagner
WHY JESUS

really last. Your efforts of obedience and humility are not only seen by God, but they are worthy in His eyes.

Holy Spirit Uncovered

"I tell you, He will see that they get justice, and quickly. However, when the Son of Man comes, will He find faith on the earth?" (Luke 18.8 NIV).

Jesus is looking for faith. If we are not believing for something by faith, we are missing out on a wonderful spiritual journey with God. God gives us promises for two reasons. 1) They will fulfill a need in the world. 2) They shape us into the image of Jesus. God's promises create an atmosphere of faith in our lives that changes us and shapes the world around us. There must always be something we are believing in according to God's will and promises. Faith becomes a lifestyle of trusting, believing and relying on God. The Holy Spirit rises up in our faith and pours out God's favor, grace and abundance into our lives when we believe God more than our circumstances. Jesus desires to see our faith, so we can begin today by believing without seeing.

Professing Prayer

"Holy Spirit, I want to cultivate a lifestyle of faith. I realize that faith opposes a world that demands proof and answers. However, I know that God is the King of the Universe, and He can make a way where there is no way.

I choose to believe according to God's promises in my life and not according to the circumstances in which I find myself."

WHY JESUS: DAY 21

Jesus Discovered

"For truly I tell you, many prophets and righteous people longed to see what you see but did not see it, and to hear what you hear but did not hear it" (Matthew 13.17 NIV).

The Old Testament prophets longed to see the promised Messiah that we have today through the life, death and resurrection of Jesus Christ. We live in the New Testament age where Jesus' blood has been shed and God's grace spread to the four corners of the earth. The world had been reconciled back to God because of Jesus' finished work on the cross. We literally live in the age of the Sabbath—Jesus has done all of the work. We receive His perfection by faith, and there is nothing we can do to earn it except to believe God at His word. The Light of Christ has been revealed on earth and in our hearts (Matthew 4.16). We can shine His glory by speaking this truth and revealing all that God has done for us and all that He shows us. We can rejoice by faith, knowing that we are living in a time that godly men and women from history's past desired to see. We no longer have Sabbath only one day a week; instead, we live in a time of the Sabbath, resting from all our human striving to be holy. Jesus has given us His holiness in exchange for our sin. We can believe and cling onto this holiness, and live our lives as an expression of love and gratitude to our Savior, Jesus Christ.

"Then the glory of the Lord will be revealed, and all people will see it together. The Lord has spoken!" (Isaiah 40.5 NLT).

Contemplative Questions

1. Can you identify areas of your life where you strive?

2. Lack of peace is the best indicator of when we are not walking in God's Sabbath Rest. Can you identify thoughts of fear, confusion and doubt and give them to God?

3. We live in the New Testament promise of redemption. How does that help you create more peace in your mind and spirit?

Faith Recovered

"Then Jesus said, 'Come to Me, all of you who are weary and carry heavy burdens, and I will give you rest. Take My yoke upon you. Let Me teach you, because I am humble and gentle at heart, and you will find rest for your souls'" (Matthew 11.28-29 NLT),

Finding rest under the shade of the Sabbath, which was bought and paid for by Jesus' finished work on the cross, takes discipline. First, we must know the truth about our freedom in Christ. Second, we must believe that we have freedom from human striving by faith. Third, we must walk in this belief rooted in truth. Faith is one of those things that takes a choice beyond human understanding. We will find that once we decide to believe God's word more than our circumstances, He will in turn flood us with His supernatural provision in response to our faith. God can and will pour out His rest upon us even in the most difficult and painful of situations, as we cry out to Him. We live in the New Testament time when God's Spirit is literally in and among us. We can recognize this truth and invite Him into our lives and every situation.

Meditation Moment

Imagine the seventh day on which God rested. He didn't need to rest, but He rested as a demonstration to you. This will be the day that Jesus takes up the mantle of work and completes the task that will save all of humanity and usher us into His rest. Walk beyond the sixth day of human striving and into the final day of rest. You are there with Christ—surrounded by His love, grace and mercy. He is always there no matter the storms around you. You can enter anytime to find rest.

Holy Spirit Uncovered

"Rest time is not waste time. In the long run, we shall do more by sometimes doing less." - Charles Spurgeon

Resting is not necessarily entertainment. Our bodies and minds are still active when we watch a movie, read a book or play a game. True resting is when we allow our bodies and minds to be still and silent before the Lord. In this day and age, rest is very hard to come by. We have our phones and computers constantly pulling at us to be active and to stay occupied. The only way we find true rest is to set everything aside and come into the presence of God. Only He can provide us with rest, and only He can quiet our minds, spirits and bodies. When all is still, we can finally hear God's voice. So many times we miss a step on our journey of faith because we weren't listening and seeing the signposts that God is placing on our paths. We must make rest a priority, so our ears will be attentive and our eyes opened to the moves of God. It may feel like it takes time away from our already busy schedule, but we will indeed save time when we discover that God always has shortcuts of grace ready for us.

Professing Prayer

"Holy Spirit, lead me each day into Your peace and rest. I don't want to live my life frantically and haphazardly. I would rather make slow steps of purpose than rushed steps of happenstance. I want to set everything aside each day and open my eyes to Your shortcuts of favor. You love me so much that You would die to spend time with me. Let me not take for granted that gift of friendship with a Holy God through the work of Jesus on the cross."

WHY JESUS: DAY 22

Jesus Discovered

"They worship Me in vain; their teachings are merely human rules" (Matthew 15.9 NIV).

We have freedom in Christ as co-heirs with Jesus and sons and daughters of the Most High King (Romans 8.17). God has lifted the rigorous laws of holiness from us by allowing His Son, Jesus Christ, to give us His perfection. As royalty, we can now focus on our personal relationship with our Heavenly Father without jumping through a bunch of hoops that would trip us up. Yes, we are going to fall and make mistakes, but as children of God through the death and resurrection of Jesus, we are instantly forgiven and continuously reconciled back to God. Once we accept Jesus as our Lord and Savior by faith, there is nothing that can separate us from God. We can free ourselves from the shackles of others and continue to show them love. If they are living burdened by rules, they will try to spread those shackles to others. We, on the other hand, will seek the Lord on all subjects—big and small—and He will show us the way, as sons and daughters of royalty.

"For God saved us and called us to live a holy life. He did this, not because we deserved it, but because that was His plan from before the beginning of time—to show us His grace through Christ Jesus" (1 Timothy 1.9 NLT).

Contemplative Questions

1. Have you experienced a time of human constraints that were traditional, not biblical?

2. Have you ever placed restrictions on yourself out of fear of others that limited your freedom in Christ?

3. How can you respond to someone's actions of insecurity and/or fear with love, rather than with offense?

Faith Recovered

"So now there is no condemnation for those who belong to Christ Jesus. And because you belong to Him, the power of the life-giving Spirit has freed you from the power of sin that leads to death" (Romans 8.1-2 NLT).

No condemnation does not mean no conviction. The Holy Spirit loves us and wants us to grow and mature into the best design that God has for us. The difference between condemnation and conviction is that one stings of death, the other rings of life. Conviction is actually a beautiful process. It shows that God loves us and He wants better for us. If He didn't care, He would simply leave us to our own destructive devices. But He does care. In fact, He loves us so much that He died for us in order to not only give us life, but to create in us the image of Himself. When we are convicted of something, we can praise God that He will give us the strength to overcome. He will joyfully walk beside us, renewing our strength the entire way (Isaiah 40.31).

Meditation Moment

Think back to a time when the Holy Spirit convicted you. He could have used a loving family member or friend to be His mouthpiece or He could have used a song, sermon or book. He could have even used the small, still sound of His voice. Instead of feeling condemned because of this correction, fill yourself up with God's love and tenderness towards you. Realize that He is convicting you because He knows your best design and He will help you walk in it.

Holy Spirit Uncovered

"Christian freedom does not mean being free to do as we like; it means being free to do as we ought." – William Barclay

Our freedom in Christ came at a dear price: the blood of Jesus on the cross. This freedom is not to do whatever we want. Left alone to our own devices, our paths will end in destruction. God has designed each of us with purpose. He has a plan for our lives that is beyond understanding. In fact, God has given us promises that we could never achieve on our own. He gives us His grace, so we can walk in the freedom of those promises. We don't have to fear. If God has given us His promise, we will accomplish them by faith as we commit to His will each day. Instead of focusing on what we want, we can allow God's will to become our will. Only then will we walk in the fullness of our purpose.

Professing Prayer

"Holy Spirit, I want to walk in the freedom of Christ. I know my utmost joy and fulfillment can only be found in the purposes that You have planned for me before time began. Give me confidence to walk in Your promises, knowing that it is only because of Your grace that I can accomplish all that You have for me."

Why Jesus: Day 23

Jesus Discovered

"Take My yoke upon you. Let Me teach you, because I am humble and gentle at heart, and you will find rest for your souls. For My yoke is easy to bear, and the burden I give you is light" (Matthew 11.29-30 NLT).

Jesus' promises can be counted on. When He says that He is "humble and gentle," He means it. And when He says that His "yoke is easy to bear," we can trust Him at His word. So why do we feel overwhelmed sometimes even though Jesus has given us these promises? God's truth doesn't change according to our feelings and it doesn't depend on our circumstances. God's truth is unchanging. When we feel overwhelmed, two things may be happening. First, we are taking on a yoke that was never meant for us. Comparison and insecurity—both linked to pride—can cause our thoughts and actions to move in ways outside of God's will for our lives. When we put our focus on others and not on Jesus Christ, we may begin to commit to and sacrifice for things that are not our burden to bear. Second, we may not be fully embracing the grace that God is giving us in our situation. God matches our heartache with His grace. This grace is supernatural and the peace we gain surpasses all understanding, but it takes faith to receive it (Philippians 4.7). If our minds are stuck on an earthly perspective and not on God's perspective, we may miss out on the grace that God is pouring out from His abundance into our hearts, minds and lives.

"For from His fullness we have all received, grace upon grace" (John 1.16 ESV).

Contemplative Questions

1. Has there been a time where you did not feel the yoke of Jesus' peace on you?

2. Taking the yoke of peace is a choice when the storms around us rage. Have you ever felt God's peace simply because you believed?

3. Describe a time when God supernaturally gave you comfort, peace and rest even though you felt like your world was falling apart.

Faith Recovered

"Jesus was sleeping at the back of the boat with His head on a cushion. The disciples woke Him up, shouting, 'Teacher, don't You care that we're going to drown?'" (Mark 4.38 NLT).

To have peace when everything is going our way is simple. To have peace when we feel like our world is falling apart is supernatural. Jesus had peace in the bottom of the boat when storms were raging all around Him. His disciples—seasoned fisherman—feared for their lives, but Jesus was in perfect peace. This peace can be ours as we let go of all our expectations and rely completely on God, trusting His plan each day. Nothing surprises God. He knows the storms that will come our way. Jesus gave us an example of how to live in a state of peace no matter the circumstances, which takes complete faith and rest in God. However, we have to let go of thinking we are entitled to be agitated, so Jesus' promise of rest can manifest.

Meditation Moment

Imagine you are in the bottom of a boat with Jesus. He is sleeping restfully and you feel drawn to sleep restfully next to Him. Envision the winds of each difficulty of your life at the moment blowing against the boat. They make a lot of noise and toss your boat around, but if Jesus can choose to have peace, so can you. Remember, there are people around you watching how you react. When you choose to trust Jesus, they see the possibility of the peace they too can have through Christ.

Holy Spirit Uncovered

"The Lord does not cause the difficulties in our lives but He does know how to take advantage of opportunities!"
– Graham Cooke

If life was just about getting saved, God would take us to heaven right when we accept Jesus as our Lord and Savior. Life is like a womb, maturing and preparing us for our forever home in heaven. Good times are fun, and God does want to bless us. But He also knows that it is the difficult times that grow us and strengthen us. When we trust God during the hard times, we choose to go deeper in the boat with Jesus where His peace is found. The greater the storm, the deeper our intimacy with Christ can become. When we have complete peace while everything is falling apart, people will begin to take notice. They will see that our reactions are guided by a supernatural power; rather than our natural circumstance. And they will want what we have in Christ.

Professing Prayer

"Holy Spirit, I want to have the perfect peace of Jesus. I choose to trust Jesus' words that His yoke is light and I can find rest in His presence. I know that the winds of circumstances blow around me, but I will not be shaken.

I know Jesus is not worried by the storm, so I will trust Him. Thank You for filling me with Your perfect peace."

WHY JESUS: DAY 24

Jesus Discovered

"And when he had come into the house, Jesus anticipated him, saying, 'What do you think, Simon? From whom do the kings of the earth take customs or taxes, from their sons or from strangers?'" (Matthew 17.25 NKJV).

The Jewish leaders of Jesus' time were constantly trying to trap Jesus in doing misdeeds. Since Jesus is the Son of God and not moved by human expectations (for He is moved by God's expectations alone), they condemned Jesus on many accounts according to their manmade rules and traditions. One rule was the temple tax. The Jewish leaders went up to Peter and asked if Jesus had paid the temple tax. Peter lied and said that He had. Peter had a weakness of caring what the religious people thought. Jesus foresaw Peter's motives and used the illustration of a king not requiring taxes from his children, only strangers. God's children are exempt from worrying about the expectations of others because we are co-heirs with Christ and children of God. However, since Jesus wants the Good News to spread, and He knows that people are easily offended, which will cause them to miss the Gospel. Jesus told Peter to pay the temple tax via a miracle of God: money showing up in a fish's mouth. As God's children, we are free from worrying about the expectations of others; but in order to prevent people from getting offended by our freedom, many times God will supernaturally provide the means to fulfill those expectations for us. We don't have to lose sleep over human rules or traditions. God will provide a way; we just need to listen to His direction and obey His plan.

"Nevertheless, lest we offend them, go to the sea, cast in a hook, and take the fish that comes up first. And when you have opened its mouth, you will find a piece of money; take that and give it to them for Me and you" (Matthew 17.27 NKJV).

Contemplative Questions

1. What are some human traditions and expectations that you have encountered?

2. The Holy Spirit gives each of us freedoms and parameters that don't contradict His Holy Word but may be specific to us. List a few of these.

3. Have you ever been hung up by someone else's freedoms? Explain a time.

Faith Recovered

"We are drifting toward a religion which consciously or unconsciously has its eye on humanity rather than on deity." – Alistair Begg

Jesus broke a lot of the Jewish laws and traditions when showing love to others. He fulfilled the law which freed Him up to live above it in order to reach people with love. God sometimes leads us onto paths that break our religious comfort zone. He wants to reach those He loves and they are usually not within the walls of our churches and home Bible studies. They are in the world desperately seeking anything to satisfy the God-sized hole inside of them. Only Jesus can satisfy the longing they are searching for, but they may not know it. They need people to walk alongside them and show them what they cannot see. When we love people, as God loves people, we will no longer be guided by human expectation or tradition. Instead, we will follow closely to where the Spirit is leading, so we can reach the lost and hurting.

Meditation Moment

Think of three people you know who need Jesus. Allow the Holy Spirit to give you a game plan. Usually reaching

people we know takes time and care. Love is always the most powerful way to reach others with the Good News of Jesus. What are some simple ways you can show love to people who need Jesus?

Holy Spirit Uncovered

"The Samaritan woman said to Him, 'You are a Jew and I am a Samaritan woman. How can You ask me for a drink?' (For Jews do not associate with Samaritans)" (John 4.9 NIV).

Jesus broke many rules when talking to the woman at the well. She was a woman and a Samaritan—both considered extremely lowly by the Jewish people at the time. Plus, this woman had a history of sexual sin. This made a triple whammy against her. Only a man pure of heart and ruled by love could talk with this woman and not become tempted with a judgmental and/or lustful spirit. Jesus brought holiness into the situation. She didn't influence Him; rather, He influenced her. How many of us are strong enough that we could transform the people and circumstances around us? God will put parameters on what we do when He knows we are weak and our maturity is lacking. However, when we are strong in Him and are completely obedient to His will, God can lead us into situations knowing that we will bring His holiness, goodness and love into the lives of the lost.

Professing Prayer

"Holy Spirit, I want to be trusted to reach the lost with the love and salvation of Jesus Christ. I know maturity takes time, and I must learn to be completely reliant on You. I ask that You mature and grow me and give me a supernatural love for Your people, so I can be an influence of good to those around me."

WHY JESUS: DAY 25

Jesus Discovered

"The wine supply ran out during the festivities, so Jesus' mother told Him, 'They have no more wine'" (John 2.3 NLT).

There are so many layers of symbolism to Jesus' first public miracle at the wedding at Cana that it would take more than one lifetime to discover all the revelation. But one of the most obvious truths gleaned from this account is Mary, Jesus' mother, had complete faith that Jesus would solve the problem. Even though Jesus expressly said that His time hadn't come and that the lack of wine wasn't His problem, Mary would not take no for an answer. She simply looked at the servants and preemptively told them to do whatever Jesus told them to do. She didn't know how Jesus was going to fix the problem, but she had absolute trust that He could and would. Most of the miracles Jesus performed were in the midst of desperation, and people pleaded with Jesus to help them and their situation. But Mary was different. She didn't plead or beg; she moved expectantly, knowing that Jesus could do the miraculous. She gave orders according to her belief in Jesus, not according to human laws of nature and physics. As Jesus' mother, she probably had a front row seat to the miracles Jesus could do. We can only wonder on what occasion Jesus supernaturally provided for His family in private. Mary knew about Jesus' giftings, and her faith in the supernatural was solid. Today, we can read about Jesus' miracles. We can read His promises in the Bible. Our faith can be just as solid as Mary's. We can move according to what Jesus can do in our desperate situation. We don't have to beg or plead; rather, we can take actions agreeing with God's promises and the supernatural power of Jesus Christ in our lives.

"But His mother told the servants, 'Do whatever He tells you'" (John 2.5 NLT).

Contemplative Questions

1. List a few small and large promises that you are believing God for.

2. What circumstances seem to be fighting against your promises?

3. How can you move by faith and work out of an expectation that Jesus can do the miraculous?

Faith Recovered

"The waters are rising, but so am I. I am not going under, but over." – Catherine Booth

Sometimes it feels like our years of faith are rising up all around us. Our long wait for God's promises is filling our lives with drops of belief that have gathered into one big deluge. God is not intending to drown us in our belief without ever seeing the fulfillment of His promises. He is allowing our faith to become as deep and wide as it can possibly get, so when He does the miraculous, everyone will see and feel the effects of His mighty hand. Just like the wedding at Cana (John 2.1-12), Jesus wants to fill as many large stone vessels with our belief as possible, so He can transform it all to new wine—His revelation poured out in our lives. We don't have to fret or succumb to disbelief. God will achieve His promises in our lives. We just need to move in belief in those promises and prepare for the outpouring of the miraculous.

Meditation Moment

Imagine yourself being surrounded by stone vessels filled with drops of your faith. They have added up over the years. You trust that Jesus will transform your work into the new wine of His grace and favor. Don't get

discouraged. Trust that God will do what He says He will do. Continue to work in the belief that Jesus can do the miraculous.

Holy Spirit Uncovered

"But He said, 'What is impossible with man is possible with God'" (Luke 18.27 ESV).

Absolutely nothing is impossible for God. He is all-powerful and all-knowing. However, His love for His people may cause His promises to feel like they tarry a bit. God dwells outside of time. Life matters more than time, so He will hold off accomplishing His promises until the full goodness of the promise can be achieved. The bigger the promise, the longer the wait and the bigger the impact. If we find ourselves waiting years or decades, we can continue to believe and move by faith. Our actions should always be motivated by God's word for our lives even when the promise seems dead. God can resurrect our dreams in an instant. And when the Holy Spirit is unleashed in our wait, God will get all the praise and glory.

Professing Prayer

"Holy Spirit, I believe all the promises You have given me, even though I've been waiting for what feels like forever. I will continue to walk and work in belief, resting in Your purpose and timing. You are all-knowing and all-powerful, so I trust You with my seconds, days, months and even years."

WHY JESUS: DAY 26

Jesus Discovered

"And Jacob begot Joseph the husband of Mary, of whom was born Jesus who is called Christ" (Matthew 1.16 NKJV).

The Old Testament was mainly written in classical Hebrew except for small portions in the books of Daniel and Ezra, which were written in Aramaic. By the time the New Testament was written, the Jewish nation was under the dominion of the Roman empire, which spoke Greek and Latin as their languages of choice. Therefore, the New Testament was written mainly in Greek because many people of the day spoke that language. It was like the English language today—a shared language that allowed people from different countries to communicate. The word "Christ" is the Greek translation of the Hebrew word, "Messiah." They both mean "Anointed One." When we read or hear the name, "Jesus Christ," we can also understand it as "Jesus, the Messiah." When the Apostle John declares Jesus as Christ, he is making a bold statement, announcing that the long-awaited Messiah—the anointed one who will usher in a time of peace and reconciliation back into God's kingdom and His heart—has finally arrived. Because of sin, the connection humanity had with God in the beginning of time was broken. What is holy cannot have anything to do with what is unholy. Yet, the Messiah would take our transgressions upon Himself and give us His perfection. Through the Messiah, God's justice and His love can co-exist. We are healed from our sinful nature through the death and resurrection of the Messiah, Jesus Christ—they are one and the same. Two expressions of the same Anointed One unite the Old and New Testaments into one miraculous picture of God's love for all His children.

"But He was pierced for our transgressions, He was crushed for our iniquities; the punishment that brought us peace was on Him, and by His wounds we are healed" (Isaiah 53.5 NIV).

Contemplative Questions

1. The Messiah is the anointed one who brings us back to God. Can you thank Jesus today for rescuing you from sin?

2. Jesus not only rescues our soul, He rescues our bodies, minds and circumstances. What are you believing He will rescue today?

3. Waiting on Jesus to move in your life can be difficult, but the wait creates faith. Can you renew your faith in His promises?

Faith Recovered

"See, I will send the prophet Elijah to you before that great and dreadful day of the LORD comes" (Malachi 4.5 NIV).

Four hundred years pass between the promise of the Messiah in the last book of the Old Testament to Jesus' birth in the first book of the New Testament. By this time, the chosen people of God, the Jewish people, have all but forgotten about God's promise to send His anointed one. John the Baptist has to become a "voice in the wilderness" to remind everyone (John 1.23). Waiting on God's promises is daunting to say the least. Sometimes, it feels like it would be easier to simply roll up His promises, throw them away and move onto something else that doesn't take so much faith. However, faith is exactly what God is trying to produce in us. Our entire life with God hinges on faith. The wait between His given word to its fulfillment is fertile ground of faith, producing His fruit in our lives. We should never give up. The burden of hope will be worth it once the Messiah finally reveals Himself in our lives.

Meditation Moment

Imagine yourself sitting in several hundred acres of barren land. You have planted many seeds, but nothing has grown yet. You look up at the skies and wait for God to send His rain. Don't move. Stay patient and trust that God will bless your obedience.

Holy Spirit Uncovered

"Faith is taking the first step even when you don't see the whole staircase." – Martin Luther King, Jr.

God's Spirit moves in our faith. And faith means we step out in obedience without knowing all the details. In fact, God may hide most of the details because He knows that if we fully understood the impossibility of the situation, we wouldn't have the faith to even begin. God is supernatural, and He is not limited to the rules of this world. He will provide for us when our faith-steps seem to leave us stranded in the wilderness. It is in the wilderness that God's power is greatly demonstrated. God wants to come through for us. We only need to take those steps of faith believing that He is stronger than our circumstances.

Professing Prayer

"Holy Spirit, no matter how long it takes, I will believe what You have spoken over me. I won't give up, and I won't let my faith be shaken. Renew my strength and direct my steps, as I protect the faith dwelling inside of me."

WHY JESUS: DAY 27

Jesus Discovered

"All those listed above include fourteen generations from Abraham to David, fourteen from David to the Babylonian exile, and fourteen from the Babylonian exile to the Messiah" (Matthew 1.17 NLT).

Numbers have meaning in the Hebrew language. God is the master writer, and everything found in His Holy Book, the Bible, has significance. A good writer never wastes a single word or number in his or her book. There are 3 sets of 14 generations leading up to Jesus' birth. The number 7 symbolizes completion, specifically Jesus' finished work of reconciling the entire world back to God. The Sabbath is on the 7th day in which we rest, knowing that Jesus Christ has fulfilled His purpose as Lord over the Sabbath. The number 14 is a double portion of this completion. So 14 generations would represent a double portion of God's completion through Jesus Christ. But God didn't just want us to have a double portion. He allowed 3 sets of 14 generations to go by before Jesus' star was seen in the sky by the three wise men. The number 3 represents many things, but when something is repeated 3 times in the Bible, it is showing emphasis on whatever is being repeated. To repeat the double portion of 14 generations 3 times is to show an emphasis on Jesus' finished work of bringing us back into God's presence. We not only get a double portion of grace through Jesus Christ, we get an emphatic double portion. It is finished! The work of staying holy before God, so we can have a relationship with Him, has been fulfilled on our behalf by Jesus Christ, the Messiah. We can put our complete faith in the cross and rest in the righteousness gifted to us by grace through the death and resurrection of Jesus, who is "holy, holy, holy!"

"Each of the four living creatures had six wings and was covered with eyes all around, even under its wings. Day and night they never stop saying: 'Holy, holy, holy is the Lord God Almighty,' who was, and is, and is to come'" (Revelation 4.8 NIV).

Contemplative Questions

1. How does the emphatic, double portion of the Good News of Jesus Christ change your perception of your daily life?

2. Have you ever said something or done something over and over again to illustrate emphasis?

3. Has there been a time in your life where God repeated something in stereo to reveal its importance?

Faith Recovered

"The Lord turned and looked straight at Peter. Then Peter remembered the word the Lord had spoken to him: 'Before the rooster crows today, you will disown Me three times.' And he went outside and wept bitterly" (Luke 22.61-62 NIV).

Peter denied Jesus three times, yet Peter is the rock on which Jesus would build His Church (Matthew 16.18). God was so merciful to Peter that even when he disowned Jesus emphatically, He still gave Peter a chance to make amends. Peter repeated that he loved Jesus three times when he repented (John 21.15-17). Peter used the forgiveness he received from God as fuel to start the vigorous work of building the church. We learn from Peter that it is never too late for us. We may have messed up emphatically, but when we finally come to Jesus, He gives us the opportunity to repent emphatically. God can always use a willing vessel to do His glorious work on earth. At any time, we can turn from our own selfish ways and come to Him. We may never be perfect, but we can remain faithful in God's love and grace.

Meditation Moment

Imagine a promise you've been waiting for as a gift-wrapped box from God. Envision Him giving you the box several times to boost your faith. Also, imagine a pain or heartache you've held onto for years. Envision laying your broken heart at the foot of the cross several times, so God can mend and repair it.

Holy Spirit Uncovered

"Forgiveness is the giving, and so the receiving, of life." – George Macdonald

Holding unforgiveness only hinders us. When we carry bitterness toward someone, we allow ourselves to become their enemy. God always deals justly with the enemy and gives mercy to the hurting. The truth is we all deserve separation from God because all of us fall short of His glory. We don't want to be dealt with justly. We want mercy. The Bible says when we give mercy, we will receive mercy (Matthew 5.7). But honestly, offering forgiveness frees us from the destructiveness of bitterness. Bitterness is literally a gateway for the enemy to tear apart our minds, emotions and bodies. It is better to forgive and to let go, so we don't set ourselves up as an enemy in God's eyes. Letting our hands go of unforgiveness gives room for us to receive from God's unending goodness.

Professing Prayer

"Holy Spirit, I'm tired of holding onto unforgiveness. Help me to offer mercy and to let go. I want my hands free to receive all that You have in store for me. I don't want to be an enemy to others—no matter what they've done to me. Show me how to give mercy, so I can receive mercy."

WHY JESUS: DAY 28

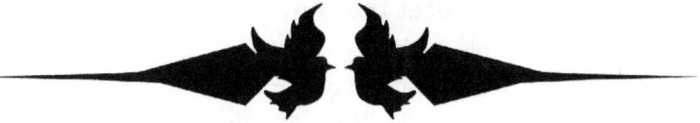

Jesus Discovered

"Now when He was asked by the Pharisees when the kingdom of God would come, He answered them and said, 'The kingdom of God does not come with observation; nor will they say, "See here!" or "See there!" For indeed, the kingdom of God is within you'" (Luke 17.20-21 NKJV).

Sometimes we are waiting for an outside situation to create an inside breakthrough, but it is the other way around. It is our faith, pouring out of a heart of belief, that alters our circumstances. Jesus explained that the Kingdom of God—God's subtle and explosive movements are inside each of us. If we want God to move in our lives powerfully, the seed of change is in our hearts and on our lips. God's best promises and His ultimate plan are available to us, but we must use our free will, yoked to the heart of God, to activate them. If we are crying out to God to change our lives, we must first allow Him to change our hearts. The Kingdom of God is unleashed from the Holy Spirit that resides in each person who has accepted Jesus Christ as Lord and Savior. That seed of salvation grows out of a spirit watered by God. This seed then sprouts and stretches to touch the lives and circumstances that surround us.

"I planted the seed, Apollos watered it, but God has been making it grow" (1 Corinthians 3.6 NIV).

Contemplative Questions

1. What outside circumstance do you want God to transform?

2. Is there a heart-shift that God desires to birth within you?

3. Instead of looking outside of yourself, how can you focus on God's love for you and His move in your life?

Faith Recovered

"Put Jesus Christ in the driver's seat of your life and take your hands off the steering wheel." – Rick Warren

Before an external breakthrough, we will contend with internal agitation. Finding peace in expectation takes trust. We must believe that God will accomplish His promises according to His timing while being patient in the wait and content in the process. This is easier said than done. The car ride to our destination is fun and full of anticipation at first, but after a long time, we will begin to ask, "Are we there yet?" However, we must remember that God is with us. He wants to get to know us. He wants to deepen our relationship with Him. We can be excited about our destination while enjoying the journey. When we finally make peace with the wait, God will unexpectedly say, "We have arrived!"

Meditation Moment

Imagine yourself in a large RV with God. Within the RV, God has provided everything you will need for the journey. Take the time during the drive to sit with God in the passenger seat. He wants to chat with you and get to know you more. There is no rush. Let Him make stops

along the way for you to behold and experience the beautiful world and life He has given you.

Holy Spirit Uncovered

"For those God foreknew He also predestined to be conformed to the image of His Son, that He might be the firstborn among many brothers and sisters" (Romans 8.29 NIV).

Before God placed our spirits in the womb of our mothers, He knew us. Now it is our time to get to know Him. Each day is filled with opportunities to get to know our Creator. He wants us to have an intimate relationship with Him because our joy is found in His presence. Moreover, God sees the best design He has for our lives. We each can be molded into the likeness of Jesus and allow God to shape us into the best version of ourselves. But the process of relationship and transformation takes time. We cannot rush the end result or we will compromise its fullness. We can have peace knowing that our highest calling—to know God and be conformed to the image of Jesus—is easily achieved each day as we seek God's face.

Professing Prayer

"Holy Spirit, guide me into a richer, deeper relationship with You. I'm tired of feeling rushed. I know You will get me to my destination, and I don't want to be anxious anymore. Help me to have peace as I trust Your direction and Your timing. Show me how to spend time with You each day during our journey, so when we finally arrive, You will have become my best friend and true love."

WHY JESUS: DAY 29

Jesus Discovered

"Think of it this way. If a father dies and leaves an inheritance for his young children, those children are not much better off than slaves until they grow up, even though they actually own everything their father had" (Galatians 4.1 NLT).

We each have God-given promises through Jesus Christ. These promises are far beyond our ability and strength to attain and maintain, so we need the grace and favor of God. However, there is also a transformation that we need to go through. God loves the process of shaping us into the image of Christ, and it is our promises that move us from Point A (reliance on ourselves) to Point B (reliance on God). We have an inheritance on earth that is ours by adoption-right as co-heirs with Christ and children of God, but God has a set time for those promises to come into fruition. When is that time? God fixed the moment on a time when He knows the promises will have the biggest impact on us and the world. He's shaping us into vessels with great capacity to overflow His Spirit. God has a masterpiece in mind for us. We have the raw material, so now we simply need to allow the Holy Spirit to mold us. There is no need to rush God. The promises are already fulfilled in the spiritual realm. He's simply preparing us and the natural world to contain them.

"Humble yourselves, therefore, under God's mighty hand, that He may lift you up in due time" (1 Peter 5.6 NIV).

Contemplative Questions

1. Do you feel God preparing you for something?

2. Do you think you are ready to usher in God's promises or do you need a little more time to prepare?

3. How can you align your faith and your actions with the promises you know God has already achieved in the supernatural?

Faith Recovered

"But when you are invited, go and sit down in the lowest place, so that when he who invited you comes he may say to you, 'Friend, go up higher.' Then you will have glory in the presence of those who sit at the table with you" (Luke 14.10 NKJV).

Learning to humble ourselves is definitely not a natural inclination. In a world that is clamoring for the highest seat, we can choose to take the lowest seat and trust that God has prepared a special place for us when the time is right. God wants to shine His glory through our lives, but He won't if He knows that our promotion will go to our heads, causing pride to corrupt our character and disrupt our destiny. Once we learn to humble ourselves and enjoy life, regardless of where we are sitting, God will set us higher. However, no matter where we are sitting in this world, we are sitting on the highest place with Christ. And no worldly seat could ever usurp God's heavenly throne.

Meditation Moment

Imagine yourself sitting next to Jesus in heaven. You are surrounded by His glory, goodness and love. No darkness, no anxiety, no worry and no fear can touch you there.

Alisa Hope Wagner
WHY JESUS

When you remember where you are sitting in the supernatural, it will help you have victory in the natural. You are seated in the highest and most precious place in all the universe. Rest there with Christ and revel in the glorious atmosphere.

Holy Spirit Uncovered

"For He raised us from the dead along with Christ and seated us with Him in the heavenly realms because we are united with Christ Jesus" (Ephesians 2.6 NLT).

If we could only see through God's eyes, we would see that no moment in time, no place on the earth and no action done by faith is insignificant. As Christians, every moment of every day is valuable and full of purpose. It may not feel like it in the natural, but we must believe that nothing is meaningless to God. Even tedious details have eternal significance when submitted to the authority and power of the Holy Spirit. We can look for the value of every second and believe that God can use all our gathered moments for His purposes and for our good.

Professing Prayer

"Holy Spirit, I know that You are with me, and I am seated with Christ in the heavenly realm. Let me never forget that You see the details of my life and they are valuable to You. I may not fully comprehend how loved and adored I am, but I want to live like each day has purpose, power and promise."

WHY JESUS: DAY 30

Jesus Discovered

"Again I declare to every man who lets himself be circumcised that he is obligated to obey the whole law" (Galatians 5.3 NIV).

Paul was pleading with the Galatians not to give in to man-made legalism that would throw them off the path of walking in righteousness gained by faith in Christ alone. Although, he was writing of "circumcision," the point is that people were trying to force these men to gain righteousness through fear of human expectation. Many Christians struggle with this form of human righteousness, trying to jump through every single religious hoop expected of them. But there is so much freedom in Christ when we lean daily on the Holy Spirit. Our freedom in Christ causes us to seek Him moment to moment, asking Him to guide us and to show us His best path. This freedom is not to do whatever we want because that will lead to destruction and confusion. The difference between what is holy and what is not is the difference between what is good for us and what is not. God cares for us and calls us out of sin because it hurts us. But God is so patient and loving that He would take each little step with us. And when we fall, He is there to love us in truth, not shame us. Nothing other than the Pierced Lamb of God gets us into the throne room and into the presence of a holy God. When we know that, we will cling solely to Him, and He will work His holiness into the rest of us little by little, making us into the people we will be for eternity.

"This righteousness is given through faith in Jesus Christ to all who believe. There is no difference between Jew and Gentile" (Romans 3.22 NIV).

Contemplative Questions

1. Have you ever felt condemned by another person's opinion?

2. How does knowing that Jesus gave you His righteousness change how you see yourself?

3. Have you been guilty of judging another person's freedom and/or their struggle?

Faith Recovered

"The 'religious spirit,' it's demonic, and it attempts to substitute a demonic power or a fleshly power for the power of the Holy Spirit. And the 'religious spirit' is more concerned with what we look like than what we really are." – Jack Deere

The religious spirit is the counterfeit of true holiness that can only be gained through the death and resurrection of Jesus Christ. The religious spirit tries to change people from the outside in, rather than the inside out. When people first come to Christ, they are in a naturally selfish state. It takes years of walking with Christ to work the supernatural holiness we gain through Christ into our hearts, minds, actions and lives. When we fear people's opinions, we may try to look like we have it all together. But as we realize that our holiness comes from Jesus alone, and it is through His finished work on the cross that we are able to have a relationship with God, we can stop keeping up false pretenses. Knowing that we are holy through Christ gives us freedom to be ourselves and helps us to rely on God's grace, not our performance.

Meditation Moment

Instead of trying to enter into a state of holiness by your own efforts, see yourself already in a state of holiness by Jesus' efforts on the cross. You are no longer striving to be holy because God already sees you as holy in Christ. Now you can make decisions and take actions out of your belief in what Jesus has already given you.

Holy Spirit Uncovered

"The next day he saw Jesus coming toward him, and said, 'Behold, the Lamb of God, Who takes away the sin of the world!'" (John 1.29 ESV).

Jesus is the Lamb of God—the payment for the world's sins, so we can have a relationship with a holy God. We have been made righteous because Jesus took our sins and gave us His holiness. It is by His sacrifice that we have access to God. Not only do we have access, but the supernatural power of the Holy Spirit resides within us. Our measly efforts at holiness could never come close to matching the holiness we have already been given. Instead of focusing on our efforts, let us focus on what Jesus has already achieved—only then can we truly let go of human expectation and walk in the freedom and authority of the Holy Spirit.

Professing Prayer

"Holy Spirit, I realize that I did nothing to deserve Your presence in my life besides confessing that Jesus is my Lord and Savior. I accept the Lamb of God as my true holiness, and I will live in full belief that I am the righteousness of God through Jesus Christ. I desire to have the power and authority of Your Spirit working within and around me."

WHY JESUS: DAY 31

Jesus Discovered

"But the fruit of the Spirit is love, joy, peace, forbearance, kindness, goodness, faithfulness, gentleness and self-control. Against such things there is no law" (Galatians 5.22-23 NIV).

When we are influenced by the Fruits of the Spirit, we are beyond reproach and the Law cannot touch us. The Fruits of the Spirit only grow where the Spirit is manifesting itself. The Law was set as parameters for our lives before Jesus Christ came to give us His holiness. Now that we have holiness through faith in the death and resurrection of Jesus, the Holy Spirit can live in us by grace. When we water God's fruit with prayer, God's Holy Word and our obedience, the full presence of the Holy Spirit becomes more powerful and more plentiful in our lives. When circumstances press down on us and people ridicule us, God's Fruit in our lives will present themselves in full force. We can't be condemned because the law cannot denounce even one of the Fruits of the Spirit. When we walk in love, joy, peace, forbearance, kindness, goodness, faithfulness, gentleness and self-control, none of the world's shame can penetrate us. We will be so full of God's Spirit and His Fruit that we will walk on a higher level above the noise and confusion below. The enemy of our souls will try to knock us down with his evil schemes, but the Fruits of the Spirit will protect us and continue to lift us up with Christ.

"So humble yourselves before God. Resist the devil, and he will flee from you" (James 4.7 NLT).

Contemplative Questions

1. What Fruit of the Spirit is having difficulty producing in your life?

2. Is there an area of your life that you haven't fully surrendered to the Holy Spirit?

3. Can you recall a time when God produced unexpected fruit in your life when you needed it most?

Faith Recovered

"This is to My Father's glory, that you bear much fruit, showing yourselves to be My disciples" (John 15.8 NIV).

Fruits of the Spirit are only grown in faith. These fruits are spiritual and are developed in difficult conditions. It's easy to have peace when the atmosphere is peaceful, but to have peace in the middle of a raging storm is supernatural. When we are confronted with challenging circumstances, we have a chance to produce more of God's fruit in our lives. It is this supernatural fruit that will make the world take notice. People will sense the realness and authenticity of God in us, and they will want what we have in Christ. We will be known by our fruit (Matthew 7.16).

Meditation Moment

Imagine a supernatural God-switch inside of you. When this switch is confronted with hate, it automatically transforms it to love. When this switch is confronted with impatience, it automatically transforms it to self-control. Think of a negative emotion you are facing right now (fear, doubt, defeat, sorrow, harshness, etc.) and allow God to transform it into something that exists in Him (courage, belief, victory, joy, gentleness, etc.).

Holy Spirit Uncovered

"Did you never run for shelter in a storm, and find fruit which you expected not? Did you never go to God for safeguard, driven by outward storms, and there find unexpected fruit?" – John Owen

No matter how hard we work, God's fruit in our lives is undeserved. It is not about earning it; rather, it is about yielding to its growth. God will match our heartache with His grace. During especially difficult trials, God calms us with His supernatural peace, fills us with His supernatural joy and empowers us with His supernatural goodness. We all have moments when God encountered our heartache so deeply that we knew it was the Holy Spirit comforting us. When we find ourselves in hard situations, we can trust that the Holy Spirit will be with us every step of the way, giving us just what we need to overcome.

Professing Prayer

"Holy Spirit, thank You for walking this life with me. I know that there is pain and heartache on earth, but I look forward to the day in heaven when every tear is wiped dry and every hurt is taken away. But until then, I open my heart and life to You, so I can have your supernatural fruit."

WHY JESUS: DAY 32

Jesus Discovered

"Then I saw a Lamb that looked as if it had been slaughtered, but it was now standing between the throne and the four living beings and among the twenty-four elders. He had seven horns and seven eyes, which represent the sevenfold Spirit of God that is sent out into every part of the earth" (Revelation 5.6 NLT).

The "Lamb that looked as if it had been slaughtered," is Jesus Christ who died for our sins and resurrected for our reconciliation back to God. The Lamb of God came to earth, claimed victory over death and bust down heaven's doors for all His brothers and sisters to enter into the holy throne room of God. Our faith sweeps us along in the wake of Jesus' grace, and we enter a perfect heaven and the awesome, powerful presence of God, our Father. It is only by the Pierced Lamb alone that we gain access to the throne room. If our confidence is in our works or in our perfection, we will never ascertain the full power of God in our lives via His grace. We can walk boldly into the throne room and God's presence because we carry the Pierced Lamb of God in our hearts and souls. Jesus is our confidence. He is our boldness. Grace is our access point, and we can make our requests known to God, rejoicing that He hears us because we have been made perfect and holy through Jesus' finished work on the cross.

"So let us come boldly to the throne of our gracious God. There we will receive His mercy, and we will find grace to help us when we need it most" (Hebrews 4.16 NLT).

Contemplative Questions

1. How will your prayer life change knowing that you can be bold before the throne of God?

2. God doesn't want you to be timid when you talk with Him. Can you come to Him with the reverence and confidence of a son or daughter?

3. When you pray with others, how will they benefit from seeing your confidence that your words are being heard?

Faith Recovered

"And we are confident that He hears us whenever we ask for anything that pleases Him" (1 John 5.14 NLT).

People need to see our confidence when we pray. Confidence in prayer takes time, especially when praying in front of others. However, we know that God hears us and He is pleased with our desire to speak with Him and to listen to His voice. We can practice praying alone, so when we are called on to pray for someone in desperate need, we can pray not necessarily with finesse, but with confidence that God truly hears us. Confidence is contagious. When we stand in the confidence that God is listening to our words, others too will have confidence. God allowed Jesus to die in order to give us access to Him and confidence as we pray. We must believe that God wants to hear us, so our confidence will spread to others.

Meditation Moment

Imagine you are walking into the throne of God to speak with Him. You are carrying the Pierced Lamb of God and He alone grants you access. No matter the mess of your human condition, your words have power and authority in the heavenly courts by the divine decree of Jesus' blood.

Holy Spirit Uncovered

"Prayer delights God's ear; it melts His heart; and opens His hand. God cannot deny a praying soul." – Thomas Watson

There is so much power in prayer. God loves us, and His Spirit lives within us. He has made communication with Him super easy, yet extremely potent. If we knew the mountains we could move with prayer, we would be praying much more in order to see heaven's agenda change the world. We not only have confidence that God hears us, but when we pray His will, we can have confidence that our prayers will be answered. God will answer our prayers in His way and according to His time. We don't have to beg God; we can simply agree with what He already wants to do.

Professing Prayer

"Holy Spirit, I know You hear me. I know that I can have complete confidence to enter the throne room of God because of the Pierced Lamb of God. Reveal Your awesome will in my life, so I can claim it and confess it back to You. I believe every promise that You are giving me."

WHY JESUS: DAY 33

Jesus Discovered

"But nothing unclean will ever enter it, nor anyone who does what is detestable or false, but only those who are written in the Lamb's Book of Life" (Revelation 21.27 ESV).

It is very difficult for a believer in Christ to truly believe he or she has been made clean by the blood of Jesus on the cross. Mistakes are still made. Struggles still persist during this life as we follow after God. But over and over again in the Bible, God's Holy Word, we are told that we have been made holy and righteous and that our sins have been cleansed. If we truly believe that we have gained access to heaven through Jesus Christ, then we must believe that we have been made clean. In the Book of Revelation, the Apostle John inspired by the Holy Spirit, says that "nothing unclean" will enter heaven. Therefore, if we claim we are going to heaven, we must also claim without a shadow of a doubt that we are no longer unclean. Supernaturally we are perfect and holy. God sees the beginning and the end simultaneously. He sees each of us walking through heaven's gates as His perfect and holy creation. We just need to get that belief based on our faith in what Jesus accomplished on the cross worked into the rest of our minds, hearts, souls and lives. The change from glory to glory begins with that belief, and it ignites our spiritual transformation on earth, causing our natural existence to catch up to our supernatural reality.

"If we confess our sins, He is faithful and just to forgive us *our* sins and to cleanse us from all unrighteousness" (1 John 1.9 NKJV).

Contemplative Questions

1. Do you truly believe that the finished work of Jesus on the cross has cleansed you completely?

2. Instead of striving to be righteous, God wants you to live from a position of righteousness. How does that knowledge change the way you believe, think and act?

3. The blood of Jesus continually cleanses you. Are you carrying the weight of condemnation even though you have been made right with God?

Faith Recovered

"For God made Christ, who never sinned, to be the offering for our sin, so that we could be made right with God through Christ" (2 Corinthians 5.21 NLT).

Jesus has done all the work of reconciling us back to our Perfect Father. There is nothing more we can do except believe and receive God's grace through Jesus Christ. We devalue Jesus' sacrifice when we don't fully trust that His finished work forgave our sins and accomplished our holiness. When we rely on our own efforts at holiness, we tell Jesus that His Sacrifice wasn't enough. Yes, it is good to live a life that pleases God out of a love for Him. However, we should live each day from a belief that we have been made righteous, not from a fear that we have to earn it. These are two opposing motives that may look similar, but they are worlds apart. When we believe that we have been given right-standing with God, our actions will be guided and moved by that truth.

Meditation Moment

If you have accepted Jesus as your Lord and Savior, you are currently in a supernaturally righteous state. Jesus' blood surrounds you, and His grace fills the crevices of your flaws and smooths the ridges of your humanity. All sin—past, present and future—has been erased. They can no longer dictate who you are and what you will accomplish. And when you stumble, you can get back up with grace and continue to walk in the confidence that your righteousness is not based on you; it is based on Jesus.

Holy Spirit Uncovered

"To be justified means more than to be declared 'not guilty.' It actually means to be declared righteous before God. It means God has imputed or charged the guilt of our sin to His Son, Jesus Christ, and has imputed or credited Christ's righteousness to us." – Jerry Bridges

Jesus was God's victory plan from the beginning. God gave us free will and He gave us Jesus. Now we can live as children of God—free to love and live for Him regardless of how much we fall short of His holy standard. Jesus has accomplished that standard for us, so love and holiness could co-exist. What freedom we have in Christ—freedom to run our race with vigor trusting that Jesus' grace will make all of our work, rest and play pleasing to God. God's Spirit is our Coach and Cheerleader directing and rooting for us. The Holy Spirit in our lives is made possible only through the sacrifice and resurrection of Jesus Christ.

Professing Prayer

"Holy Spirit, thank You for always guiding me. Even when I go my own way for a bit, You are right there waiting for me to return to You. I feel You cheering me on. I hear Your voice proclaiming my victory. And I trust that You will accomplish through me all that You have planned since before I was born."

WHY JESUS: DAY 34

Jesus Discovered

"As Isaiah said, 'Rejoice, O childless woman, you who have never given birth! Break into a joyful shout, you who have never been in labor! For the desolate woman now has more children than the woman who lives with her husband!'" (Galatians 4.27 NLT).

Paul recites a verse from the Old Testament found in Isaiah 54. He is discussing two different ways to gain God's promise: One, we can attempt to achieve our promise by force and human ingenuity. Two, we can patiently receive our promise by resting and waiting for God's supernatural provision. This is the choice that Abraham was confronted with and failed the first time; but, thankfully, God's promises are based on His faithfulness, not ours. Abraham birthed two sons: one spawned out of performance and the other out of promise. Eventually, the son birthed outside of God's will was cut away from the promised son, Isaac. We may feel "barren" for a time as we wait on God, but we must always trust in His faithfulness to be true to what He says—we will give birth to our promise. If God accomplished His promise of a Savior, He can easily accomplish all other promises. We must resist the urge to take over the process of our promise coming to fruition or it will not be established in God's supernatural power and favor. But if we let God's process and timing take over, He will carry and maintain our promise in His mighty strength, blessing it with His abundance and goodness.

"But what do the scriptures say about that? 'Get rid of the slave and her son, for the son of the slave woman will not share the inheritance with the free woman's son'" (Galatians 4.30 NLT).

Contemplative Questions

1. Have you ever tried to force the fulfillment of God's promises instead of waiting on His timing?

2. Has there been a promise in your life that God has accomplished? Is there a promise for which you are still waiting?

3. Is there any area of your life where you need to let go and let God have control?

Faith Recovered

"Once I knew what it was to rest upon the rock of God's promises, and it was indeed a precious resting place, but now I rest in His grace. He is teaching me that the bosom of His love is a far sweeter resting-place than even the rock of His promises." – Hannah Whitall Smith

God's promises are beautiful. The most precious of them is reconciliation through Jesus Christ. However, these promises are not an end in themselves. They are merely the catalyst for God's love. God promised a Savior because He knew that only through Jesus would we be able to rest in His love. Sometimes, we can get so fixated on God's promises and their fulfillment that we forget to rest in His absolute love for us. God wants to have a relationship with us. It is because of His great love that He created us and died for us. Our desire for God's promise should never overshadow our desire for His presence. God wants to wrap us up in the divine romance of His love—everything else is simply the overflow.

Meditation Moment

Imagine an ocean dotted with beautiful, lush islands. One island represents God's promises. Another island represents God's goodness. Yet another island represents

God's provision. However, there is a great island in the center of the ocean that represents God's love. This island has everything the other islands have combined into one. Find rest on the Island of God's Love, and you will have everything you need and more.

Holy Spirit Uncovered

"So we have come to know and to believe the love that God has for us. God is love, and whoever abides in love abides in God, and God abides in him" (1 John 4.16 ESV).

"God is love" is the truth that all existence rests upon. God is a creator because He is love. God is a savior because He is love. God is a father because He is love. God is a healer, lover, counselor, encourager—all because He is love. If we fully understood just how much God loves us, we would see every day as a gift to both love and be loved. God created us, so we could be a part of His grand love story. He has so much love in who He is that He created people in His image in order to offer them His love. Through Jesus Christ, we can have this love. The Holy Spirit is God's Spirit in us and all around us. We have access to God's Spirit 24 hours 7 days a week. There is an endless supply of love that God has for us if we would only learn to receive it.

Professing Prayer

"Holy Spirit, teach me how to rest in Your love even more. I desire Your presence more than the promises You have for me. Forgive me for allowing myself to get so lost in the plans of my destiny that I neglected resting in Your love."

Why Jesus: Day 35

Jesus Discovered

"Don't cling to Me," Jesus said, "for I haven't yet ascended to the Father. But go find My brothers and tell them, 'I am ascending to My Father and your Father, to My God and your God'" (John 20.17 NLT).

Jesus was a physical being who walked this earth. People got to see, hear and touch Him. He was human and had the power to heal the sick, raise the dead and even forgive sins. Yet, this power He demonstrated during His short three-year ministry on earth was nothing compared to the power He would pour onto the earth through the Holy Spirit after His ascension to the Father in heaven. Mary Magdalene clung onto the old Jesus, the one she could see, hear and touch, and Jesus told her to stop. She wanted to encapsulate her relationship with Him in a natural and temporal way. Yet, He was about to multiply Himself on the earth and in the hearts of His people in a supernatural and divine way. Mary needed to make the transition from Jesus the Teacher to Jesus the Savior. She had to let go of the "Seed of David," that had been broken and buried in the ground. The seed now transformed into a great crop of forgiveness, mercy and love that was spreading across space and time. And that crop continues to multiply new seeds into the hearts, minds and souls of us and all the generations to come.

"Remember that Jesus Christ, of the seed of David, was raised from the dead according to my gospel" (2 Timothy 2.8 NKJV).

Contemplative Questions

1. Have you ever wished you could see, touch and talk to the physical Jesus?

2. The Bible says that we are all members of Christ's body (1 Corinthians 12.27). Does knowing we can be His hands and feet to the world give you a sense of connectedness to Him?

3. One day, we will see Jesus face to face in heaven. What will be the first thing you do or say to Him?

Faith Recovered

"It is not great talents God blesses so much as great likeness to Jesus." – Robert Murray M'Cheyne

When we feel like Jesus is very far away, we can have peace and joy in the fact that God is creating us to be the very likeness of Christ. Jesus is not so distant as we may assume. He is part of the Holy Trinity, communing with God the Father and God the Holy Spirit. Plus, Jesus intercedes on our behalf continuously (Romans 8.34). We might not be able to cling onto Him as Mary Magdalene once did, but even she had to allow Him to go to the Father to make room for the Holy Spirit. Jesus walked this earth, He touched lives and He extended love to the world. He is still doing this today through each one of us. When we interact with others like Christ, we are literally being the presence of Jesus in their lives.

Meditation Moment

Imagine Jesus in your mind. He is there next to you. Talk with Him. Let Him know your struggles and pain. Thank Him for dying on the cross for you. Fill your mind and heart with communication with Christ by faith. One day you will see Him face to face, and He will have all of your conversations saved.

Holy Spirit Uncovered

"And if I go and prepare a place for you, I will come back and take you to be with Me that you also may be where I am" (John 14.3 NIV).

Jesus is coming back for His bride, the church. We will either be on the earth when He arrives or we will already be in heaven. Either way, we are going to Jesus, and we want to invite as many people to join us as possible. God took Jesus to heaven, so He could send His Spirit on the earth. God's Spirit is with us, and He wants us to reach more of His children with the Good News of Jesus Christ. God doesn't want any of His children to be separated from Him, but it is only through Jesus Christ that we can have a relationship with God. This is our time to share God's love to the people around us. The Holy Spirit within us calls out to them. We can be a mouthpiece for Christ, letting everyone know that Jesus is preparing a place for His beloved people.

Professing Prayer

"Holy Spirit, guide me as I engage others about the love of God through Jesus Christ. Sharing my faith can be a scary prospect because I know some people will reject me. But they are not really rejecting me; they are rejecting Christ. Open their hearts and minds to the Gospel, so I can bring as many people to heaven as possible."

WHY JESUS: DAY 36

Jesus Discovered

"She replied, 'That's true, Lord, but even dogs are allowed to eat the scraps that fall beneath their masters' table'" (Matthew 15.27 NLT).

The Gentile woman's daughter was sick. She knew that Jesus was the Son of David, the promised Savior to the Jewish people and the world. She knew He could perform miracles. She knew that He could save her daughter's life. But God has a process for everything, and Jesus' earthly ministry was geared towards His people, the Jews. It would be the Apostle Paul and others like him who would bring the Good News to the rest of the world. But this woman was undeterred. She had so much faith in Jesus and what He could do that it usurped who she was and the cultural biases towards her as a Gentile, a woman and an outcast. Jesus tested this faith, cultivating it and making it ignite within her. She had a head knowledge of who Jesus truly was, but He wanted that knowledge to permeate into her actions, her determination and her persistence. Jesus called out the faith within the people

He encountered. He looked within their souls and tested their belief, causing their faith to either rise up or fade away. The woman would not give up because she knew that His mercies were not based on who she was. They were based on who He was—the Son of God who is full of love and mercy and who willingly gave His life to save the world. Claim the miraculous mercies of Jesus today—mercies that have nothing to do with us, and everything to do with Him.

"'Dear woman,' Jesus said to her, 'your faith is great. Your request is granted.' And her daughter was instantly healed" (Matthew 15.28 NLT).

Contemplative Questions

1. How has God tested your faith? Did your faith rise up or diminish?

2. God's "scraps" are still better than anything the world can offer us. Is there something of the world you're hanging onto that is preventing you from reaching for what God has to offer?

3. Have you given up on any of God's promises for your life? How can you persist in belief knowing that your faith pleases God?

Faith Recovered

"But Jesus looked at *them* and said to them, 'With men this is impossible, but with God all things are possible'" (Matthew 19.26 NKJV).

Nothing is impossible for God. However, His ways are higher than our ways (Isaiah 55.9), so His plan and timing will be different than what we envision. Sometimes planning every detail sets us up for heartache and failure. We have our agendas and schedules, but they probably don't correlate with God's. Instead of focusing on the details, we can trust that God sees the bigger picture, and He knows every single detail. As we can seek Him every day, He will show what we can accomplish according to His will that day. He usually doesn't give us the complete blueprint of His master plan because that would prevent us from having faith. God wants us to love Him with all our heart and trust Him with the details of our lives.

Meditation Moment

Imagine a divine blueprint with all the details of your life according to God's plan. The blueprint is much too complicated for you to understand because it encompasses all of history and your integral purpose in His masterplan. But God offers you a small flashlight and allows you to see the step right in front of you. If you accomplish daily what He has called you to do, you'll have a profound impact upon the blueprint of God.

Holy Spirit Uncovered

"God knows what each one of us is dealing with. He knows our pressures. He knows our conflicts. And He has made a provision for each and every one of them. That provision is Himself in the person of the Holy Spirit, indwelling us and empowering us to respond rightly." – Kay Arthur

We can get bombarded with worry when we take our focus off the provision of today and try to evaluate the lack of tomorrow. The Holy Spirit is fully aware of our needs and desires. And He is not surprised by the issues we are dealing with. We can go to Him and give Him all of our worries, doubts, frets, heartaches and struggles. He loves us so much that He wants to carry those burdens for us. If God wants us to take a step of obedience or a leap of faith, He will highlight the course we need to take. As long as we are submitted to Him, we have nothing to fear.

Professing Prayer

"Holy Spirit, I'm tired of worrying and fretting about the future. I trust that You are fully capable of providing for me, and You will show me the steps I need to take as they come. I know that You are empowering me with everything I need to accomplish Your will today."

WHY JESUS: DAY 37

Jesus Discovered

"Isn't it enough for you to keep the best of the pastures for yourselves? Must you also trample down the rest? Isn't it enough for you to drink clear water for yourselves? Must you also muddy the rest with your feet? Why must my flock eat what you have trampled down and drink water you have fouled?" (Ezekiel 34.18-19 NLT).

When Jesus washed the disciples' feet, He was not just making an example of being a servant. He was showing them and all of us that there are some things only Jesus Himself can do. One of those things is washing our metaphorical feet after we have traveled in His service for a time. When we stay obedient to Jesus, love always usurps tradition. We will follow Jesus into the sorrows and heartaches and sins of others because He longs to reach them. As we do this, we will see, hear, feel and experience the dirt of this world. We are clean because we are washed by the blood of the Lamb, but our feet become dirty from doing ministry and loving others. We can't expect others to wash all the grime off our feet. Jesus is the only one who can thoroughly purify our hearts, minds and souls from the filth of the world that we walk through in order to reach the lost and hurting. We must sit in His presence and allow Him to identify the dirt and wipe it clean. Otherwise, we can muddy the water of the people in our sphere of influence. We can carry grudges or stained attitudes that affect our walk of faith. Let us sit with Jesus today, and ask Him to cleanse the dirt of ministry away.

"Jesus replied, 'A person who has bathed all over does not need to wash, except for the feet, to be entirely clean. And you disciples are clean, but not all of you'" (John 13.10 NLT).

Contemplative Questions

1. Have you ever experienced the filth of the world when you were trying to show the love of Jesus to others?

2. If you feel like your feet are dirty and you're muddying things up with your attitude, will you allow Jesus to clean your feet and cleanse your heart and mind?

3. Will you ask God to expose any dirty areas that you might be holding onto?

Faith Recovered

"Does God ask us to do what is beneath us? This question will never trouble us again if we consider the Lord of heaven taking a towel and washing feet." – Elisabeth Elliot

God loves His lost children, and He will ask us to go places outside the church walls in order to reach them. We may feel uncomfortable at first, but we must learn to be a light in the darkness. We can bring heaven to people who don't know it exists. We can introduce people to Jesus who don't know who He is. As we travel the darkness to reach people, nothing is too lowly if love is our motivator. However, as we see and experience things that manifest in the darkness, we will eventually have to return to the safety of God's arms. This is where we can allow Jesus to cleanse us of any bitterness, attitudes or compromises we have been exposed to while spreading the Good News of Jesus Christ.

Meditation Moment

Imagine Jesus kneeling before a large basin of soapy water. There is a towel around His waist, and He's waiting for you to dip your weary feet into the warm, cleansing liquid. Now envision Him washing your feet clean. All the

bitterness, negativity and compromises of the world are gone.

Holy Spirit Uncovered

"But if we walk in the light, as He is in the light, we have fellowship with one another, and the blood of Jesus, His Son, purifies us from all sin" (1 John 1.7 NIV).

It is in the darkest places that the light is really visible. When we feel overcome with the darkness around us, we can tap into the light of the Holy Spirit within us. We can sing praises to God. We can read our Bible. We can thank God for His goodness. The Bible says that God inhabits the praises of His people (Psalm 22.3). The best way to fight the darkness is to praise God. The Holy Spirit will powerfully manifest when His name is being praised. Once we have allowed the Holy Spirit to shine through us, we can find rest in Him.

Professing Prayer

"Holy Spirit, I don't want to be so distant from You that I'm unable to distinguish light from dark. I want to shine brightly and not allow the darkness to cause my light to fade. I know You want to be strong in and through me. I will praise Your name, so everyone can see Your presence in my life."

WHY JESUS: DAY 38

Jesus Discovered

"And yet, O LORD, You are our Father. We are the clay, and You are the potter. We all are formed by Your hand" (Isaiah 64.8 NLT).

We are the masterpiece of God our Father in heaven (Ephesians 2.10). Everything we do in submission and obedience to Him is beautiful no matter how we perceive it. Doing the dishes as a service to our family is just as awe-inspiring as teaching a Bible study for our church. If they are both done in accordance to the Holy Spirit, they are both stunning strokes of paint on the canvas of our lives. So many times, we want our days and moments to be filled with epic actions and grand circumstances, and we may look down on the normal, day-to-day activities of service to our family, others and God. But God has placed us in a life that will be filled with both the extraordinary and the ordinary. We can't avoid the "small" things that we are called to do and expect God to bless the "big" things. A blessed relationship is built on both small and big things. An anointed ministry is established through small and big things. And a life dedicated to God will also be shaped by the small and big things. God can and will use us according to His kingdom plan, which will entail both the authority and humility of the Gospel. Jesus not only spoke from the mountain top, He also got on the floor and washed feet. We must never forget that as we minister to God and others, we will find ourselves on the mountain and the floor. They are both important because they each give depth and richness to our life of faith.

"When a potter makes jars out of clay, doesn't he have a right to use the same lump of clay to make one jar for decoration and another to throw garbage into?" (Romans 9.21 NLT).

Contemplative Questions

1. Are there small activities that you do in your daily life that cause you to grumble and complain?

2. When God calls you to serve Him on the mountain top, do you struggle with fear or pride?

3. Who are the people you serve that you have no expectation of repayment?

Faith Recovered

"The measure of a man's greatness is not the number of servants he has, but the number of people he serves." – John Hagee

To be served is childlike because we take from our lack. To serve is godlike because we give from our abundance. Many times God will have us give from our lack to show us that His provision is always within us. Often, we don't want to give because we feel we don't have enough. Then we hoard the little we do have fearing we will run dry. However, God never runs dry. And if we have His Spirit within us, we can tap into that unlimited source. God wants us to learn to rely on Him and His abundance. So let us serve and give from our lack, trusting that God will pour out His blessings in and through us. We will never run out or run dry as we trust in Him.

Meditation Moment

Imagine the Holy Spirit within you as a continuously burning flame. You may be weak, but the flame is strong. You may be confused, but the flame is sure. You may have lack, but flame has abundance. Don't focus on the world to provide for your needs and fulfill your dreams. Rather, look to the flame of God who gives from His unlimited supply.

Holy Spirit Uncovered

"Yet it shall not be so among you; but whoever desires to become great among you, let him be your servant" (Matthew 20.26 NKJV).

Jesus' view of how to live is polar opposite of the world's view. The kingdoms of this world are limited and finite, but God's kingdom is limitless and eternal. Jesus showed us how to live in His upside down kingdom—the greatest being the servant—but He didn't leave us to navigate this truth alone. The Holy Spirit is our constant supply. Once we trust that God's Spirit has an overflow of all our needs and of those needs around us, we will begin to rely on Him. When we struggle with lack in our minds, hearts, bodies and lives, the Holy Spirit within us has just what we need each day. We can claim His provision instead of looking to the world to fulfill our needs. As we care for others, we can trust that God will care for us.

Professing Prayer

"Holy Spirit, I trust that You have everything I need each day. Show me how to rely on this truth. I want to always look to You first when I have a lack, heartache or longing. You are in me, guiding my path and providing along the way."

WHY JESUS: DAY 39

Jesus Discovered

"I will bless My people and their homes around My holy hill. And in the proper season I will send the showers they need. There will be showers of blessing" (Ezekiel 34.26 NLT).

Hills and mountains in the Bible—both New Testament and Old Testament—represent a place of worship and of drawing nearer to God. Ezekiel prophesies in the Old Testament that those who establish their lives on God's "holy hill" will receive "showers of blessings." There is a hill mentioned in the New Testament that releases the blessings of God within. The word *Calvary* and *Golgotha* come from the Greek word, *Kranion*, which means *skull*. When we picture the image of a skull on land, we see the presence of a hill. This Hill of Calvary is where Jesus Christ was crucified for the sins of all humankind, so we would be reconciled back into a relationship with God. It is on this hill that we are able to worship God and draw closer to Him. Just like a geyser, we are able to tap into peace, love, joy and hope that is not based on our circumstances. These "showers of blessings" are based solely on God and His goodness extended to us. So when we feel dry and in desperate need of God's blessings, we must remember the holy hill of Jesus Christ and establish our lives on it. Only there can we have God's goodness flowing over us.

"When they came to a place called The Skull, they nailed Him to the cross. And the criminals were also crucified—one on His right and one on His left" (Luke 23.33 NLT).

Contemplative Questions

1. The skull is a symbol of death, yet through Jesus' sacrifice so much life has been saved. What symbol of death has God been able to transform in your life?

2. Do you have a "hill" or place in your home that you worship God?

3. Jesus sacrificed His life in order to achieve something better for humanity. What sacrifice has God asked you to make, so He could bless you with better?

Faith Recovered

"You are the light of the world—like a city on a hilltop that cannot be hidden" (Matthew 5.14 NLT).

Jesus says we are "like a city on a hilltop." Our bodies now carry the Spirit of God because of what Jesus did for us on the cross. We can worship God at any time—rain or shine—throughout every moment of the day. When we worship God, our joy is made complete because only He is worthy of worship. When others see us worshiping God—not people, things or situations—they will have a front row seat to watching lasting joy unfold. Everything on earth will disappoint us and let us down, but God will never let us down. Yes, He allows us to live in an imperfect world for a time, but His goodness could never be squelched in a heart receptive of Him.

Meditation Moment

Imagine yourself on a hill—you are on a place of worship. At any moment throughout your busy and hectic day, you can stop and worship God from this hill. As you worship Him, you will be filled with His peace, joy, goodness, strength and provision. Come to this hill whenever you feel like you are lost or running on empty.

Holy Spirit Uncovered

"Christ in the heart of every man who thinks of me, Christ in the mouth of everyone who speaks of me, Christ in every eye that sees me, Christ in every ear that hears me." – Saint Patrick

Do people see Christ in us—or at least something that is not of this world and they can't explain? There should be a marked difference in every Christian. As we walk with God, He is molding us into our best selves—the image of Christ in us. When people think of us, Jesus should automatically rise into their thoughts. Everywhere we go, we can exude the scent of Christ—His love, His forgiveness, His mercy and His goodness to the world. For it is Christ who opens the way for the Holy Spirit to shine brightly in our lives. As we live for Jesus, let others see His love, goodness and character in our daily lives.

Professing Prayer

"Holy Spirit, I realize that it is Jesus who ushers Your presence and power into my life. I want the fullness of God's Spirit flowing through me, so I will unashamedly proclaim Jesus to the world. When people are with me, I want them to sense the presence of Jesus in my life."

Why Jesus: Day 40

Jesus Discovered

"There I will make the horn of David grow; I will prepare a lamp for My Anointed" (Psalm 132.17 NKJV).

The horn is symbolic of strength. This strength can be used in alignment with God (for good) or in alignment with ourselves (for evil). Prophets in the Bible would use a horn to store anointing oil. When God was about to move His Spirit within people, they would be anointed with oil from a horn. The oil represents the Holy Spirit being poured out onto a person's life. Today our Horn of Strength is Jesus Christ. He died, was buried and rose again, so He could take the sting of death from all who accept Him. Jesus ascended like a Horn, so that the Holy Spirit could be poured out onto the world. This great anointing shows us today that God's Spirit is moving within the lives of His people. The flow of oil is free and abundant to anyone who carries the Horn of David within their hearts.

"And you know that God anointed Jesus of Nazareth with the Holy Spirit and with power. Then Jesus went around doing good and healing all who were oppressed by the devil, for God was with Him" (Acts 10.38 NLT).

Contemplative Questions

1. Jesus is your Horn of Strength. How does this truth help you deal with the stresses and difficulties of every day?

2. Do people sense a strength in you that comes from a supernatural source?

3. Does knowing that the King of Kings and Lord of Lords is your strength help alleviate your worries and fears?

Faith Recovered

"For the Spirit that God has given us does not make us timid; instead, His Spirit fills us with power, love, and self-control" (2 Timothy 1.7 GNT).

Jesus is compared to a horn only once in the Bible in Psalm 132.17. However, the promise of His strength found within this metaphor is for all of us who recognize it and claim it. We can be strong in our faith because Jesus is our Horn of Victory. We can walk in an authority that is not our own because Jesus has given us His. Despite what the world says, we are always victorious in Jesus. The horn can be used as a weapon or it can be used as a call to action. Jesus is our power and defense, and He is our mouthpiece calling others to "fight to the good fight of faith" (1 Timothy 6.12 NKJV).

Meditation Moment

Imagine a large ox horn at your side. At any moment you can use this weapon to fend off the attacks of the enemy. There is a power that exudes from this horn that knocks all evil down with one fling. But when you feel overwhelmed by the enemy's tactics, you can use this horn to call for help.

Holy Spirit Uncovered

"When a man has no strength, if he leans on God, he becomes powerful." – D.L. Moody

The Holy Spirit is our daily strength. When we are bombarded with feelings of inadequacy, defeat and doubt—we simply need to allow the Holy Spirit to take over. God's Spirit has infinite power and endless strength, and He wants to carry us through the difficult times. He is simply waiting for us to let go and reach for Him. When we surrender to God, we now have His strength fighting for us and providing for our every need. Becoming like a child before an all-powerful Father is an act of faith that releases the Holy Spirit in our lives and situations. Nothing could be stronger than admitting we need help from our mighty God.

Professing Prayer

"Holy Spirit, You are my strength and my protector. I submit to You because only by You will I have complete victory over my enemies. I give You access to my life, and I choose to rely on Your mighty power and strength."

WHY JESUS: DAY 41

Jesus Discovered

"But the jar he was making did not turn out as he had hoped, so he crushed it into a lump of clay again and started over" (Jeremiah 18.4 NLT).

There are two types of jars seen in the Old Testament. Jars are symbolic of earthen vessels, which are God's children on earth wrapped in flesh. Jars are made of the earth, and we have been made of the earth (Genesis 3.19). God tells Jeremiah to go to the potter's house to see what can happen to the jar that is pliable in God's hands. Jeremiah sees the potter working on the jar, but the jar is flawed. The potter instantly crushes the jar and begins to rebuild it. The first type of jar is flawed but pliable and can still be used by God. Next, God shows Jeremiah the hard jars. When crushed, these jars fall to pieces. Jeremiah takes these jars to the garbage dump, and he destroys them. The pieces of these jars are scattered and cannot be rebuilt. The second type of jar is flawed but hard and cannot be used by God. All of us are flawed. The only difference between being used by God and not being used is whether or not we are sensitive to His Spirit. Pliable jars are humble. Hard jars are prideful. We will never be perfect, but God can shape our lives into something beautiful as we stay humble and pliable in His hands.

"As these men watch you, Jeremiah, smash the jar you brought" (Jeremiah 19.10 NLT).

Contemplative Questions

1. Has God ever allowed you to be crushed by circumstances?

2. When crushed, were you resilient to the Holy Spirit or did you allow your faith to be destroyed for a time?

3. Was God able to rebuild your life after devastation because of tenderness of your heart toward Him?

Faith Recovered

"And I will give you a new heart, and I will put a new spirit in you. I will take out your stony, stubborn heart and give you a tender, responsive heart" (Ezekiel 36.26 NLT).

We cannot renew our hearts without the Father's help. He promises that He will take out our dead, stony heart and give us a new, tender heart. Life is not fair, and we experience things that can cause us to be jaded or bitter. But when we harden our hearts, we prevent the love and tenderness of God from flowing freely in our lives. Many of us have allowed our hearts to become so hardened that we don't even know how to begin to soften it. We don't have to put our hearts under a heat lamp or try to soak it in a hot bath. We simply need to ask God to take away our old heart with the pains of the world scarring it and replace it with a new heart with His signature of love written across it.

Meditation Moment

Imagine your bruised, stony heart. It gets very little blood flow because it has become too hard. Now offer that heart up to God. He takes your old heart into His mighty palms and hides it under gentle fingers. Then His hands reveal your heart once more. But instead of bruised and hard, it looks pink and soft. He gives it back to you, and you feel the blood pumping freely.

Holy Spirit Uncovered

"Forgiveness is the economy of the heart. Forgiveness saves the expense of anger, the cost of hatred, the waste of spirits." – Hannah More

Forgiveness is the quickest way to prevent our hearts from becoming hard. People will disappoint us. Life will let us down. And our own desires can play tricks on us. But God's love is forever. Since we are so loved, we can freely offer forgiveness in order to keep our hearts pliable to God and soft towards others. The Holy Spirit can only move powerfully through a tender heart that is beating for Him. Holding grudges only stops the flow of God's goodness in our lives. Unforgiveness only hurts us in the end, and it is not worth carrying. Once we finally let go of anger that can lead to hatred, our spirits will feel as light as a morning breeze on a spring morning.

Professing Prayer

"Holy Spirit, highlight any grudges that I have been holding onto. I know they are weighing me down and hardening my heart. I want my life to feel free again like a little child. I want to be aggressive about forgiving others, so I can have Your Spirit flowing in me."

WHY JESUS: DAY 42

Jesus Discovered

"Now it was the Preparation Day of the Passover, and about the sixth hour. And he said to the Jews, 'Behold your King!'" (John 19.14 NKJV).

Pilate is being forced to declare judgment on Jesus because of the angry crowd of Jews forming at his doorstep. They wanted Jesus crucified because He was the King of the Jews by their own declaration, so they could crucify Him. Jesus' kingship had two realities: the temporal and the eternal. His kingship on earth from the time He was declared King by Pilate to the time He died on the cross is estimated to be around three hours. Jesus was declared the King of the Jews by Pilate at the 6th hour (12pm) and died on the cross around the 9th hour (3pm). Jesus has the shortest recorded kingship in all of the Bible. However, Jesus' fleeting temporal kingship on earth is the humble key to His everlasting kingship that encompasses all of history and eternity. The counterfeit perspective to Jesus' reign is a sad, short story of disgrace and weakness. But the true perspective of His reign is one of strength, love and grace. Jesus took our punishment of death and gave us His gift of everlasting life. He lived a perfect life, forfeiting His righteousness to make us holy, so we could have a relationship with God. The crucifixion can be seen as something horrible or remarkable, depending on the view we choose to take. We must look at every situation through God's eternal view of truth. Even though our circumstance may appear to be one of humiliation and limitation, we can trust that God is using it as a key to unlock His power, victory and glory in our lives.

"Now from the sixth hour until the ninth hour there was darkness over all the land" (Matthew 27.45 NKJV).

Contemplative Questions

1. Have you ever experienced God's transformation of your humiliation into His glory?

2. Is there a situation in your life that seems humble, but you know God has called you there?

3. Sometimes victory is on the other side of struggle. What are you going through right now that you can claim God's victory over?

Faith Recovered

"Defeat in doing right is nevertheless victory." – Frederick W. Robertson

Jesus' death on the cross seemed like defeat to so many. However, we know today that His sacrifice was not a failure. Rather, it was an astounding victory that has transformed all of history. Jesus' supposed "defeat" reconciled the entire world back to God. Often times, God may have us make decisions or take actions that seem to lead us straight into defeat, but we can trust that our obedience to His will always leads to victory— regardless of how the world sees it. Just like Jesus' death on the cross, God can take what looks like an injustice and transform it into our triumph. We shouldn't run away from defeat because God can produce springs in the desert and provide miracles in the wilderness (Isaiah 41.18).

Meditation Moment

Think of an injustice that has been done to you. Now imagine God transforming that heartache into a powerful force to spread His love, forgiveness and mercy to the world. Trust that God has saved each of your tears (Psalm

56.8), and that He will create beauty from the ashes of your life (Isaiah 61.3).

Holy Spirit Uncovered

"He generously poured out the Spirit upon us through Jesus Christ our Savior" (Titus 3.6 NLT).

The Holy Spirit has been "generously poured" out onto the earth through the death and resurrection of Jesus Christ on the cross. And this Spirit continues to pour out onto every area of our lives that we submit to God's will. If God is calling us into hardship or asking us to take a risk, we can believe that God's Spirit will go before us and remain with us. What seems like a loss or like a setback is actually a chance for God to demonstrate His resurrection power in our lives (Ephesians 1.19-20). Nothing done out of obedience is a loss. Everything God wills has purpose. We can be confident in our steps of faith despite the outcome.

Professing Prayer

"Holy Spirit, I want to trust Your guidance regardless of the end result. I believe that You know what You are doing, and I won't question when I feel like my obedience has led me into what appears to be a brick wall. I have faith that nothing is impossible for You to resurrect or to transform."

WHY JESUS: DAY 43

Jesus Discovered

"And all the people answered and said, 'His blood *be* on us and on our children'" (Matthew 27.25 NKJV).

Pilate is trying to release Jesus because he believes that Jesus is innocent. Yet, the mob demands that He be crucified. Pilate symbolically washes his hands in water to show the people that he would not be accountable for the death of an innocent man. This is when the people cry out, "His blood be on us and on our children!" It is ironic that they were claiming Jesus' blood on them and their children because that is exactly what Jesus died to do. His blood is the essence of living water (God's Holy Spirit) mixed with flesh (Jesus is Immanuel, God with us). His blood was poured out onto a corrupt world making it perfect and new once more, so we could be reunited back to God. The cries of the crowd were blood-thirsty— people desperately, yet unknowingly thirsting for their Father's love and presence. Their hearts were angry, but they were also desperate, lost and confused. Jesus understood this. He knew that once His blood was indeed on the people and their children, they would be brought back into the Father's heart. Even though their cries were full of hate, Jesus would exchange their hate for love and their punishment for mercy.

"He is so rich in kindness and grace that He purchased our freedom with the blood of His Son and forgave our sin" (Ephesians 1.7 NLT).

Contemplative Questions

1. Have you ever been so ruled by hate that you cried out something that you regretted later?

2. Examine a time you spoke in anger. Were you actually speaking out of hurt, pain or fear?

3. How can trusting God help you to not sin when you find yourself angry?

Faith Recovered

"Anger is short-lived in a good man." – Thomas Fuller

Sometimes people and situations can cause us to feel angry. But instead of allowing the anger to fester within us, we can see it as a chance to come to God. God understands how we feel about the wrongs that occur in this life. He knows that things on earth are unfair, but His perfect kingdom plan can still be accomplished in a corrupt world and through imperfect people. We can instantly go to God in prayer and open His Holy Word to find clarity and peace during confusing and difficult times. The abundance of His goodness is always available to us. Let us not be too busy to seek Him when emotions try to take over our lives. In an instant, God will ease our hearts and minds with His presence.

Meditation Moment

Imagine sticky globs of emotional goo trying to attach themselves to you. Someone at work talks about you—glop! The news overwhelms you—glop, glop! Your hard work was rejected—glop again! All of these negative situations seek to smother you with destructive thoughts. Fall before God and allow Him to take every one of those sticky globs off of you, so you can be free to enjoy the beauty of the day He has gifted you.

Holy Spirit Uncovered

"If you are angry, do not let it become sin. Get over your anger before the day is finished" (Ephesians 4.26 NLV).

God does not get offended by our anger when it concerns the things He cares about. Our love for God and others will create a passion to see justice and truth prevail. In those situations, we can take our anger to God and allow Him to motivate us to action—turning our anger into fuel for good, not evil. However, sometimes our anger can be rooted outside of love. This anger is powered by insecurity, bitterness, jealousy or pride. This form of anger is rooted in sin and should immediately be captured and given to God (2 Corinthians 10.5). No matter what causes our anger, the Holy Spirit is there to help us work through it. If God commands us to get over our anger by the end of the day, then He will help us to accomplish that command.

Professing Prayer

"Holy Spirit, show me if my anger is rooted in love or sin. If it is rooted in love, tell me what I should do about it. If it is rooted in sin, take it away from me, for I do not want to harbor evil. Most of all, help the anger to be gone before I lay down to bed, so it won't rob my peace and steal my joy."

WHY JESUS: DAY 44

Jesus Discovered

"Jesus replied, 'Blessed are you, Simon son of Jonah, for this was not revealed to you by flesh and blood, but by My Father in heaven'" (Matthew 16.17 NIV).

Today we have the Holy Spirit in us to reveal God's truth to us each day. We can listen to sermons, read books and watch seminars that encourage us, but we are truly blessed when we listen to what the Father in heaven wants to say to us directly. Peter most likely watched Jesus pray to the Father. He saw as Jesus heard from God directly. And Peter, too, began to listen. And, of course, the Father always wants to reveal more about His Son, Jesus. Jesus asked His disciples what others were saying about Him. Then He asked His disciples what they themselves thought of Him. This is when Peter confidently declared what he had heard from God: "You are the Christ, the Son of the living God." This was a very bold statement—one that would eventually cost Peter his life—but this truth had been revealed to him by God Himself. Those truths we hear directly from God can and will change us and our lives. It is what God reveals into our spirit that causes us to give up everything in order to pursue the promises He has for us. Motivation and positivity can only move us so far, but one single revelation from God can move mountains and change destinies. This is why we must seek God every day, keeping our hearts attentive to His presence and our ears attentive to His words. And when we have lost all courage, all energy and all strength to continue our walk of faith, we can sit still, wait and listen for God to speak to us again.

"So God set another time for entering His rest, and that time is today. God announced this through David much later in the words already quoted: 'Today when you hear His voice, don't harden your hearts'" (Hebrews 4.7 NLT).

Contemplative Questions

1. What revelation has God shown you that is confirmed in His Holy Word?

2. Why is hearing revelation from God directly more powerful than hearing revelation from others?

3. Sometimes, we are spiritually weak and must rely on others to speak God's words over us. Have you experienced a time when God sent just the right word through others?

Faith Recovered

"You know your mind is renewed when the impossible seems logical." – Bill Johnson

Renewing our minds in Christ allows us to perceive and receive the great revelatory insights of God. We have to sit before God and strip away every distraction that tries to take precedence. Then we can open ourselves up to really hear from Him. A relationship with God is not one way. He wants to listen to us speak, but He also wants us to listen to Him speak. He has profound truths that He delights in sharing with us as His children. There are spiritual forks in the road ahead of us that veer away from the normal way of doing things. We will be prepared for the new direction God has for us and ready to shift into supernatural gear only when we learn to hear the voice of God and listen to what He has to say.

Meditation Moment

Take time to really sit with God. He adores spending time with you, and He loves sharing the details of His kingdom plan to those willing and able to listen. Learn to pull your heart and mind away from all the world's distractions, and simply allow your mind to be a blank notebook for the hand of God to write upon.

Holy Spirit Uncovered

"But it was to us that God revealed these things by His Spirit. For His Spirit searches out everything and shows us God's deep secrets" (1 Corinthians 2.10 NLT).

The Holy Spirit is the embodiment of God within us. He has all the goodness, knowledge and power of God in Him, and His presence resides in us because of the finished work of Jesus on the cross. We do not have to feel lost, lonely or confused. And if we are struggling with feelings of doubt, we can sit before the throne of God and allow the Holy Spirit to speak to us, guide us and empower us. God has secrets that are kept for those who are eager enough to seek and hear them. They are there for all of us who will take the time to spend with God and get to know His voice. The Spirit of God is truly a gift in our lives—a gift that we should prioritize using.

Professing Prayer

"Holy Spirit, I don't want to neglect spending time with You. You have all the answers, provisions and goodness I need. If I am feeling worn down or confused, I know that it is time to sit with You. Don't let the busyness of the day cause me to forget how valuable and precious is my time with You."

Why Jesus: Day 45

Jesus Discovered

"For no other foundation can anyone lay than that which is laid, which is Jesus Christ. Now if anyone builds on this foundation *with* gold, silver, precious stones, wood, hay, straw, each one's work will become clear; for the Day will declare it, because it will be revealed by fire; and the fire will test each one's work, of what sort it is" (1 Corinthians 3.11-13 NKJV).

If we tried to build our foundation (our lives) on anything or anyone other than Jesus Christ, our work will not produce eternal fruit. We may see a lot of glittery gold and jewels in our lives on earth and in the world's eyes, but God sees beyond the temporal and into the eternal. Anything that is not rooted in the vine of Christ will not transfer from this life to the next because it has not been redeemed through His blood. Only efforts found in Christ will be lasting because He is able to bring them from death to life through His resurrection power. Sometimes obeying God seems humble and plain at first, but when we see from heaven's perspective, we see the sapphires and rubies that God sees. God promises in His Holy Word that if we build our lives on Jesus Christ, believing His best and submitting to His will, our lives will be beautiful. The Bible uses the metaphor of a wondrous building to explain what God sees when we submit to Him. He is building us like castles made of gems and crystals and other precious stones, holding eternal value and purpose.

"O you afflicted one, tossed with tempest, *and* not comforted, Behold, I will lay your stones with colorful gems, And lay your foundations with sapphires. I will make your pinnacles of rubies, Your gates of crystal, And all your walls of precious stones" (Isaiah 54.11-12 NKJV).

Contemplative Questions

1. Have you ever built your life on something other than God, like work, relationships or ministry?

2. How does knowing that nothing can be eternal unless it is rooted in Christ help you to seek God's will in all the details of your life?

3. Before you make a decision or take a step, can you ask God's will to ensure your actions are eternal?

Faith Recovered

"Anyone who listens to My teaching and follows it is wise, like a person who builds a house on solid rock" (Matthew 7.24 NLT).

Wisdom is knowing that we don't know anything at all and seeking out the One who does know. Jesus gave us many teachings that are written in the New Testament. However, the entire Bible declares His name. Jesus stands in the center of space and time, holding together the past and future, and heaven and earth with the feet and hands that were nailed to the cross. Only when we build our life on Him, will we have the security of heaven, the peace of God and the love of a Savior. If we aim to understand anything, it would be to comprehend the depth of God's love for us, and that this love is made possible only through the finished work of Jesus Christ. Once we know how much we are loved by God, we will want to build our lives on nothing other than Jesus.

Meditation Moment

Imagine a house that represents you. It can be any size, any color and any style. Once you are done creating your metaphorical house, envision it resting securely on a large, solid rock. This rock represents Jesus. No matter the storms that come, the earthquakes that rumble or the wars that rage, the rock of Jesus cannot be moved.

Holy Spirit Uncovered

"One day in God's grace is equivalent to a thousand days of striving by your own effort." – Joseph Prince

Human striving is exactly what the enemy wants us to do. The devil wants us to get so distracted trying to do everything in our own human strength and understanding that we are too busy to go to God. Our lives become bogged down with busyness and we wonder why we have lost our joy. The word, *grace*, comes from the Greek word, *charis*, which means many things, including, *joy, pleasure, delight, good-will* and *favor*. God has so much grace that He wants to extend to us. He loves to bless us and surround us in His atmosphere of joy, pleasure and delight. He can accomplish more in a second than we can in a lifetime, but we must learn to come to Him first. We can't let the inevitable thorns of responsibility choke out our time with God (Matthew 13.7). God is our first priority. Once we understand that, our joy will return and we'll have time to accomplish each day's responsibilities.

Professing Prayer

"Holy Spirit, I realize how important it is that I come to You each day. I know that my days are busy, and You enjoy that I work. But I should never let my work take away from my time with You. When I come to You, I open the way for Your grace to flood my life."

WHY JESUS: DAY 46

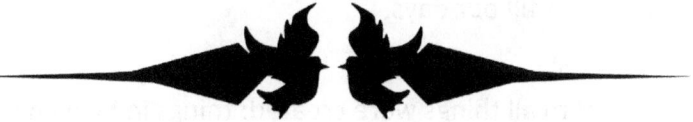

Jesus Discovered

"O LORD, what a variety of things You have made! In wisdom You have made them all. The earth is full of Your creatures" (Psalm 104.24 NLT)

In Psalm 104, God is organizing and defining all of creation. He's telling the waters where to stay. He's bringing forth the mountains and trees. He's setting the moon and sun to mark the seasons. He's creating order, so life can have peace and abundance. So many people want peace and abundance in the world, but we struggle with allowing God to create order in our own lives. God has His best design for us that will promote peace and abundance, but we have to let Him in, let Him work and let Him lead. His parameters for us are for our good, well-being and purpose. They are not to limit us; they are to empower us. Jesus is the mouthpiece of God to us. He has already perfected us through His grace, but we need to work that perfection into our daily thoughts, decisions and actions. We can allow Him to organize our lives one day at a time. Even when it doesn't make sense now, we can trust that eventually we will see the masterpiece He is creating. If Jesus can organize the world and all its intricate systems, He can organize our lives and all of the details that fill our days.

"For in Him all things were created: things in heaven and on earth, visible and invisible, whether thrones or powers or rulers or authorities; all things have been created through Him and for Him" (Colossians 1.16 NIV).

Contemplative Questions

1. Is there a change that God wants to make in your life?

2. Have you experienced a time of great change when God was rearranging your beliefs, actions and life?

3. Sometimes change just happens because life on earth is not perfect. How has God walked with you through change that you didn't want?

Faith Recovered

"Imagination must constantly run on a new track or it becomes lifeless. A living imagination is essential to prayer." – Calvin Miller

God has an infinite imagination. He created the animals in the air, land and sea with His imagination and spoke them into being with His words. Changes are very difficult to make if we can't imagine them. If we allow our limited experience and knowledge to dictate the order of our lives, we will never grow into the fullness that God has ordained for us. When we feel stuck, it is probably because our imagination cannot envision what God has for us next. That is when we need to rely on God's imagination to show us what He is envisioning for us. Once we see His awesome picture for our lives, we can then start to speak and claim what He envisions. We can only live out what we can see, so let us allow our imagination to live in the heavenly places with God.

Meditation Moment

Sit with God and allow Him to take the limited viewpoint you have gained in life thus far. Allow Him to breathe His imagination onto your heart, mind and soul, so you can comprehend the great plan He has for you in full color.

Alisa Hope Wagner
WHY JESUS

Once you can see all the promises He has in store for you, you can begin to claim them with your words and actions of faith.

Holy Spirit Uncovered

"Have I not commanded you? Be strong and courageous. Do not be afraid; do not be discouraged, for the LORD your God will be with you wherever you go" (Joshua 1.9 NIV).

Change can be scary, especially if we've never been that way before. Yes, we can ask God to give us a vision of what He has planned for us, but in the end, we are going to have to take a leap of faith. Our trust in God must overshadow our fear of the unknown. God commands us to be strong and courageous, and He cannot command anything that is impossible. Thankfully, if God commands something and we are unable to produce it, He will fulfill it on our behalf. The Holy Spirit is with us always, giving us the strength and courage we need. We may still be afraid, but we will never be alone. We have a divine comforter with us—who is guiding, teaching and walking with us.

Professing Prayer

"Holy Spirit, I no longer want to let fear of change prevent me from allowing God to organize my life into its highest and best design. I'm tired of being discouraged by worry of failure. I know that You are with me, so I have nothing to fear. And if I do stumble and fall, You will be right next to me to pick me up and help me to stay on the course."

WHY JESUS: DAY 47

Jesus Discovered

"In the beginning was the Word, and the Word was with God, and the Word was God. He was with God in the beginning. Through Him all things were made; without Him nothing was made that has been made" (John 1.1-3 NIV).

Language allows us to share our thoughts, feelings and lives with other people. Whether we use spoken words or hand gestures, we feel connected with others when we communicate. People who are new to a language may feel very isolated if they are unable to speak with the people around them. Being acknowledged and understood is one of the basic aspects of being alive. Without language we feel alone. The Bible says Jesus is the "Word of God." He is the Holy Word communicating connectedness within the Holy Trinity (God, Jesus and the Holy Spirit). He is also the Holy Word communicating connectedness between God and His people. Jesus is God's mouthpiece telling all of us that we are loved, we are valuable and we are worth dying for. Just before

Jesus died on the cross, He declared, "It is finished" (John 19.30). What He communicated at that great moment was that His blood shed for our sins had become words of grace spreading all over the world. Through Jesus, we have powerful words that we can claim every day: "Death has no sting" (1 Cor. 15.55). "We are forgiven" (Matt. 26.28). "We are righteous" (Romans 3.22). "We are God's children" (1 John 3.1). "We are co-heirs with Christ" (Romans 8.17). Jesus died to give us these words, so let us live in their truth and declare them as ours.

"He is dressed in a robe dipped in blood, and His name is the Word of God" (Revelation 19.13 NIV).

Contemplative Questions

1. Do you find yourself communicating the enemy's lies or God's truth more?

2. How will daily Bible reading change how you believe, what you think and the words you say?

3. Have you ever been lost on what to pray? Will you read the Bible and simply read back the promises God has already given you?

Faith Recovered

"Our confession will either imprison us or set us free. Our confession is the result of our believing, and our believing is the result of our right or wrong thinking." – Kenneth E. Hagin

Words are so powerful, but before we can utter mighty words, our belief system must be aligned with God's Holy Word, the Bible. We truly don't realize how skewed our belief system is and how limited our words are until we read the Bible every day. As we read God's Holy Word, our belief system begins to go through metamorphosis—changing from a worldly perspective to a heavenly perspective. Our thoughts will change, our words will change, our actions will change, and eventually our lives will change. Change starts from the inside out. If we try to change our circumstances first, we will only lapse back into old habits. First, we can change our thinking, then we can change our lives, and finally we can change the world around us.

Meditation Moment

Imagine your existence divided into five sections from: 1) you have your belief system. 2) you have your thoughts. 3) you have your spoken words. 4) you have your actions.

And 5) you have your life. Instead of trying to change number 5 first, go back to number 1. The only way to change your belief system is to fill your heart and mind with the Bible and biblical resources, and faith-filled people, music, ministries, etc.

Alisa Hope Wagner
WHY JESUS

Holy Spirit Uncovered

"I will study Your commandments and reflect on Your ways" (Psalm 119.15 NLT).

Not only can we meditate (think or reflect) on God's Holy Word, we can meditate on His ways. Because of Jesus, we have the Holy Spirit's movements on earth and in our lives. He is all around us moving through people, nature and circumstances. The Holy Spirit wants us to listen to His voice and perceive His ways. If we look closely, we can see Him in the lives of those who love Him. We can hear Him in a song. See Him in a good deed. Watch Him in a mother's caress. Or experience Him on a beautiful day. His awesome actions are all around us. He provides the rain, creates the waves and shines the moon. He is speaking to us as He moves across the earth. He is here today with us flowing with the ebb and flow of life. If we don't stop and reflect, we will miss so much of what He's trying to tell us.

Professing Prayer

"Holy Spirit, I don't want to miss another move of Your love, compassion and mercy on this world. I know You are all around me, shining God's glory on the earth. Help me to perceive Your movements. I want to reflect not only on Your words but on all Your ways. I want to know Your movements so intimately that I sense instinctively when You are up to something."

WHY JESUS: DAY 48

Jesus Discovered

"Suddenly, there was a sound from heaven like the roaring of a mighty windstorm, and it filled the house where they were sitting" (Acts 2.2 NLT).

After Jesus' resurrection, He promised the disciples that the Holy Spirit would come on them with power. Isn't it interesting that the Holy Spirit first descended in a home? From the home, the disciples moved to the streets and then the synagogues. I don't think it's a coincidence that Satan attacks our homes more than anything because that is the place—in the ministry of family—that the Holy Spirit will pour out and spill into the lives of our communities and churches. Within the ministry of the mother and father, the sister and brother and the daughter and son is where God will truly ignite His power like dynamite. The first four disciples Jesus called were brothers. God the Father, God the Son and God the Holy Spirit are a triune family. God loves family! So many times we are busy with everything but our families, and we leave our homes to the wayside to pursue more public platforms. God will extend our public platforms, but He will hold us back until the ministry of family is a strong foundation from which He can ignite His movements. The stronger the foundation, the bigger the structure God can build in our lives. Jesus wants to demonstrate His glory in and through us, but not until He lays a firm family foundation.

"Enlarge your house; build an addition. Spread out your home, and spare no expense! For you will soon be bursting at the seams. Your descendants will occupy other nations and resettle the ruined cities" (Isaiah 54.2-3 NLT).

Contemplative Questions

1. Has the ministry of the home been a priority to you or have you neglected its purpose and power?

2. Why would God want you to have a secure family life before He unleashes your public life?

3. Are you serving in a capacity that is not done in public? Do you believe that God will bless what is done in secret?

Faith Recovered

"It is amazing to me the number of people who will volunteer to help at church but won't lift a finger to help at home!" – Joyce Meyer

When we easily volunteer for public service but neglect to serve in the privacy of our home, we may need to check our motives. Are we serving to please God or people? Are we being motivated by obedience or by a desire to be recognized? Doing something "good" for the wrong reason will cause our work to be rooted in pride, not the vine of Christ (John 15). Anything not rooted in Jesus will never be eternal. God loves family. He desires us to care for the people He has entrusted to us—moms, dads, siblings, children, friends, neighbors, teachers, first-responders, etc. We can ask God what we can do to bless the people around us without expectation of repayment, recognition or reward.

Meditation Moment

What can you do to bless and serve the people you love? Write down a list of names, and ask God how you can bless each one of them in secret. Even small things, like baking cookies, writing a letter or mowing the lawn can make a profound impact. You will never know how one

act of kindness can change the course of that person's life, allowing them to feel loved, valued and appreciated.

Holy Spirit Uncovered

"Give your gifts in private, and your Father, Who sees everything, will reward you" (Matthew 6.4 NLT).

God's rewards are so much better than any reward people can offer. God rewards include things that money cannot buy—love, peace, joy, contentment, purpose, hope and satisfaction. Plus, He has heavenly rewards for everything we have done on earth in obedience to His Spirit (Revelation 22.12). We may not know exactly what God's reward will be, but we can trust that He is a good Father who has the world's resources at His disposal. There is nothing God can't do. However, having a relationship with God through the finished work of Jesus is our most precious reward. We can't earn or deserve this reward because it is a free gift to those who ask for it. All other rewards are nice, but the Gift of Salvation is everything. You can share this Gift with the people you love, so they too can have salvation and a relationship with a holy God.

Professing Prayer

"Holy Spirit, having You is a gift, and I want to share You with the people I love. I know that I could only have Your presence in my life because of Jesus, so I want to tell others about Jesus by my actions and words. Let me shine the light of His love to those around me, so they too can accept His gift of salvation."

WHY JESUS: DAY 49

Jesus Discovered

"Therefore, if anyone is in Christ, the new creation has come: The old has gone, the new is here!" (2 Corinthians 5.17 NIV).

"Wite-out" is used on paper to cover up mistakes people make when writing or typing letters. This white paste is able to hide the old ink, so something new and correct can be written over the error. Even though the mistake is covered, the deficiency is still obvious to the readers. They see the white paste and note that something incorrect was once written there. Jesus did not go to the cross to merely "wite-out" our sins. He died and rose again to completely eradicate our sins. His blood doesn't just cover up, it infuses into our lives and makes us new. The word, *justified*, comes from the Greek word, dikaiōsis, which describes the act of God removing guilt. The blood of Jesus Christ lifts the ink of our sin from the pages of our lives—not even the imprint of our mistakes can be seen in His eyes. He took our sin with Him into death, and He left them in the tomb. He achieved victory over death, and He rose back to life so that we could have victory with Him. If we accept Jesus as our Lord and Savior, the pages of our lives will be perfect and blameless—a masterpiece of God's words written across our life on earth. No mistakes. No corrections. A seamless life lived for God.

"Therefore, since we have been made right in God's sight by faith, we have peace with God because of what Jesus Christ our Lord has done for us" (Romans 5.1 NLT).

Contemplative Questions

1. Do you still hold onto past mistakes as if God can still see their imprint on your life?

2. Clinging onto what's already been forgiven can weigh you down and distract you from achieving God's best. Will you let go of everything that God no longer sees?

3. People may remind you of old mistakes because they are having trouble moving on. Will you gently remind them of God's forgiveness and how it completely removes sin?

Faith Recovered

"It is your passion that empowers you to be able to do that thing you were created to do." – T.D. Jakes

We are new creations in Christ, and because of this we are fully capable of achieving every single promise that God has given us. We each have been created to do great things. God doesn't make mistakes, and He designs everything with meaning and value. We can seek out our purpose in God and become passionate about all that He wants to do in and through us. Letting go of our old nature and claiming our new nature in Christ is the first step towards achieving our destiny. We have to envision the path that God has for us—even when we can't see all the details. Then we can take a faith-risk, empowered by our passion to live for God, and begin our journey to our Promised Land.

Meditation Moment

Imagine your Promised Land far in the distance. This land calls out to you. You know the path will be difficult and you will need help along the way, but you feel the Holy Spirit with you, preparing you and cheering you on. God doesn't make mistakes. He poured purpose and worth into you. Now it is time to claim your promises, knowing that you'll be transformed into the image of Jesus along the way.

Holy Spirit Uncovered

"In the same way, the Spirit helps us in our weakness. We do not know what we ought to pray for, but the Spirit Himself intercedes for us through wordless groans" (Romans 8.26 NIV).

We each have strengths and weaknesses. Our strengths we can handle, but it is our weaknesses we tend to avoid. But the Bible says the Holy Spirit's help can be found in our weaknesses. It is in our struggle that we tend to cry out to God for help and rely on His strength. The Holy Spirit is not surprised by our lack, and He's not deterred by our flaws. In fact, He knows exactly what we need and when we need it. He has the supply already available to us—even when we ourselves don't know what we are missing. We can trust that the Holy Spirit is speaking to God on our behalf. He is our traveling partner to the Promised Land. He's there to guide us through the winding pathways and helps us in times of trouble. We only need to rely on Him.

Professing Prayer

"Holy Spirit, I don't want to miss the destiny to which God has called me. With Your help, I know I can accomplish my part in God's kingdom plan. Thank You for praying for

WHY JESUS

me when I don't know what to do, where to go or what to ask for. Guide me on this life-journey. I am relying on You to get me to my Promised Land."

WHY JESUS: DAY 50

Jesus Discovered

"Then one of the elders said to me, 'Do not weep! See, the Lion of the tribe of Judah, the Root of David, has triumphed. He is able to open the scroll and its seven seals'" (Revelation 5.5 NIV).

Two metaphors used to describe Jesus are the lion and the lamb. The lion is fierce and strong, and it has no natural predators. The lamb, on the other, hand would never make it alone. It needs human intervention just to survive. Jesus allowed Himself to be led like a lamb to the slaughter. He placed His life willingly into the hands of humanity, and we brought Him straight to the cross. Some might think Jesus showed weakness, but in actuality Jesus' humility unto death is the strongest demonstration of love on earth and heaven. Jesus willingly gave His life, took the sins of the world and allowed Himself to be forsaken by God—all because He loved us. The Lion became the Lamb to forgive us of our sins and bring us back to God. This beautiful contradiction reminds us that we should never look at

God's move with earthly eyes. What seems weak or humble to us, may actually be powerful and awesome.

"As Jesus walked by, John looked at Him and declared, 'Look! There is the Lamb of God!'" (John 1.36 NLT).

Contemplative Questions

1. How has God demonstrated His glory in your life or the lives of the people you love?

2. Have you experienced the beautiful contradiction of the lion and the lamb personally? In what way?

3. Jesus is our Great Sacrifice, allowing us to be reconciled back to God in a loving relationship with Him. Can you thank Jesus today for all He has done?

Faith Recovered

"Have you been asking God what He is going to do? He will never tell you. God does not tell you what He is going to do; He reveals to you who He is." – Oswald Chambers

God has an ultimate kingdom plan that includes all of us in it, but most importantly, He wants to get to know us as His children, and He wants to be known as our Loving Father. Sometimes we can be more motivated by achieving God's will than actually getting to know Him intimately. The sole purpose for which He created us was to know Him and be known by Him. He wants to bring us into His love, which is why Jesus died on the cross to take our sins and give us His righteousness. Now we can finally have a relationship with God even in our imperfect state. Each new day is a chance to get to know our Heavenly Father. God is good, and He knows we have responsibilities and things to do. He knows we want our lives to have value and meaning. He also knows that our greatest joy comes from spending time with Him.

Meditation Moment

Sit with God today. Bring nothing but yourself. Come exclusively to spend time with Him. You can ask Him questions and pray about your needs later. But right now,

Alisa Hope Wagner
WHY JESUS

just come to Him and allow Him to fill you with His thoughts, His love, His grace, His comfort and His peace.

Alisa Hope Wagner
WHY JESUS

Holy Spirit Uncovered

"So if you sinful people know how to give good gifts to your children, how much more will your heavenly father give the Holy Spirit to those who ask Him" (Luke 11.13 NLT).

The Holy Spirit is the gift to the world, bought and paid for by the blood of Jesus Christ on the cross. This Gift came at a high price—God's Son—and we have this gift available to us at any moment of each day. The Holy Spirit is the person of the Trinity that dwells among and in us. The Holy Spirit is our counselor, teacher, comforter, healer, provider, cheerleader, motivator and supporter. He is the power and goodness of God who produces supernatural Fruits of the Spirit within us. He waters our souls with living water, He prunes our hearts with His gentle hand and He gives us clarity with the Mind of Christ (1 Corinthians 2.16). Everything we need to live a life that pleases and glorifies God is found in the Holy Spirit. We simply need to ask for more of Him in our lives.

Professing Prayer

"Holy Spirit, I want the fullness of You in my life. I see my need for You. I know that only in You will I have victory over my days. You are my gift from God that came at the price of His Son. I will no longer ignore or neglect this gift. I will see You daily and allow You to have free access to all of me."

Alisa Hope Wagner
WHY JESUS

I pray this book has blessed you. Toward the end of writing it, I felt completely poured out with nothing left to offer. However, every time I sat down at the computer, the Holy Spirit would flow from my heart, to my fingertips, to the keyboard and onto the screen. I didn't have to worry because God wanted the book written more than I did, and He knew exactly what He wanted to say.

Thank You, Holy Spirit, for choosing an imperfect vessel to share Your love and truth!

If you enjoyed this book, might I ask that you leave a review on Amazon? I would love to know how the Holy Spirit touched your life through these pages. And make sure to check out my YouTube channel (my handle is @alisahopewagner) to watch my short *Why Jesus* videos for each of the 50 days.

With love,
alisa

www.ingramcontent.com/pod-product-compliance
Lightning Source LLC
Chambersburg PA
CBHW071303110426
42743CB00042B/1160

Alisa Hope Wagner
WHY JESUS

I pray this book has blessed you. Toward the end of writing it, I felt completely poured out with nothing left to offer. However, every time I sat down at the computer, the Holy Spirit would flow from my heart, to my fingertips, to the keyboard and onto the screen. I didn't have to worry because God wanted the book written more than I did, and He knew exactly what He wanted to say.

Thank You, Holy Spirit, for choosing an imperfect vessel to share Your love and truth!

If you enjoyed this book, might I ask that you leave a review on Amazon? I would love to know how the Holy Spirit touched your life through these pages. And make sure to check out my YouTube channel (my handle is @alisahopewagner) to watch my short *Why Jesus* videos for each of the 50 days.

With love,
alisa